Emerging Biology in the Early Years

This inspiring text celebrates young children as 'emergent biologists' and explains how their natural inquisitiveness and curiosity can be harnessed to increase early understanding of scientific concepts, and so lay the foundations for future learning about the living world.

Full of practical tips, suggested discussion points and hands-on activities, *Emerging Biology in the Early Years* is a uniquely child-focussed resource. Chapters provide key information on the physical environment, including weather phenomena and soils, plants, animals and human development, and prioritise the child's perspective to offer activities which are in line with their natural development, thereby provoking discussion, problem-solving and child-led investigations. From planting seeds, to classifying rocks, flowers and animals, to understanding growth processes and recognising anatomical features, this book takes a holistic approach to science which moves beyond the confines of the curriculum and the classroom and shows how biology can be taught in a fun, engaging and inexpensive way both at home and in the early years setting.

Providing a rich collection of ideas, activities and downloadable sheets, this will be an invaluable resource for early years practitioners and parents looking to develop young children's scientific skills and understanding.

Sue Dale Tunnicliffe is a Reader in Science Education, a biologist, former teacher and a researcher at the Department of Curriculum, Pedagogy and Assessment at the UCL Institute of Education, University College London, UK.

Emerging Biology in the Early Years

How Young Children Learn About the Living World

Sue Dale Tunnicliffe

LONDON AND NEW YORK

First published 2020
by Routledge
2 Park Square, Milton Park, Abingdon, Oxon OX14 4RN

and by Routledge
52 Vanderbilt Avenue, New York, NY 10017

Routledge is an imprint of the Taylor & Francis Group, an informa business

© 2020 Sue Dale Tunnicliffe

The right of Sue Dale Tunnicliffe to be identified as author of this work has been asserted by her in accordance with sections 77 and 78 of the Copyright, Designs and Patents Act 1988.

All rights reserved. No part of this book may be reprinted or reproduced or utilised in any form or by any electronic, mechanical, or other means, now known or hereafter invented, including photocopying and recording, or in any information storage or retrieval system, without permission in writing from the publishers.

Trademark notice: Product or corporate names may be trademarks or registered trademarks, and are used only for identification and explanation without intent to infringe.

British Library Cataloguing-in-Publication Data
A catalogue record for this book is available from the British Library

Library of Congress Cataloging-in-Publication Data
Names: Tunnicliffe, Sue Dale, author.
Title: Emerging biology in the early years : how young children learn about the living world / Sue Dale Tunnicliffe.
Description: Milton Park, Abingdon, Oxon ; New York, NY : Routledge, [2019] | Includes bibliographical references and index.
Identifiers: LCCN 2018060191| ISBN 9780815377108 (hb : alk. paper) | ISBN 9780815377115 (pb : alk. paper)
Subjects: LCSH: Nature–Study and teaching (Early childhood) | Nature study–Activity programs.
Classification: LCC LB1139.5.S35 T849 2019 | DDC 372.21–dc23
LC record available at https://lccn.loc.gov/2018060191

ISBN: 978-0-8153-7710-8 (hbk)
ISBN: 978-0-8153-7711-5 (pbk)
ISBN: 978-1-351-23474-0 (ebk)

Typeset in Bembo
by Swales & Willis, Exeter, Devon, UK

Visit the eResources: www.routledge.com/9780815377115

In memory of Ann Wright, a friend and fellow biologist, Professor at Canisius College, Buffalo, New York, who died young, August 2016, after a brave fight before we could write this book we planned.
Sadly missed.

Sue

Contents

List of figures		viii
List of tables		ix
Introduction		1
1	Beginning to learn about the living world	4
2	Learning about ourselves	14
3	Learning about other animals	25
4	Learning about plants	42
5	Observing changes in living things	60
6	Naming living things	86
7	Earth science: Rocks, soil, weather and habitats	104
8	Interactions between physical science and living things	129
	Index	145

Figures

2.1	Tadpole man drawn by a 4-year-old boy	15
3.1	A butterfly drawn by a 5-year-old girl from Brazil	32
3.2	The outside of an insect drawn by a 5-year-old boy from Brazil	34
3.3	Drawing by an 8-year-old boy showing the inside of an earthworm	36
3.4	Drawing of a fish by a pre-school-aged boy from Brazil	38
3.5	An 11-year-old pupil's drawing of the internal organs of a bird	38
3.6	Drawing of a dog	39
4.1	Child's drawing of a 'lollipop' tree	54
5.1	Life cycle summary	61
7.1	The central place of Earth science in our living world	105
7.2	A simple rock identity chart	115

Tables

2.1	Analysis criteria for the presence of organs	18
2.2	Definition criteria for organ systems	18
2.3	A summary of the levels, organs and systems obtained by the children	19
2.4	Summary of scores from drawing a kidney by the seven children who were still at this school at the end of their primary education	20
2.5	A summary of organs and systems mentioned overall by the seven children	21
4.1	Initial discussion about plants	53
4.2	Responses to plants	54
4.3	Level source of knowledge about trees as shown in drawings	56
5.1	Seed length, colour and shape	69
5.2	Tracking absorption of water by seeds	73
5.3	Observations of a growing seed	74
5.4	Comparison of growing seeds in warm and cold environments	76
5.5	Length of foetus during pregnancy	83
6.1	What's my name?	94
7.1	Collecting and observing pebbles	114
7.2	The weather and what I wore	116
7.3	My weather symbols	118

Introduction

This book was written for a friend with whom I often discussed the need for such a book. Sadly, after developing leukaemia, she died in 2016 and I decided that I must try to write this book on her behalf.

After 50 years in education I have found the answer to a question that I asked myself when I began teaching girls studying for the A-level zoology exam in an English grammar school. The question being: where, I pondered, had they acquired their knowledge of the subject which they brought to our lessons? I wondered the same about the younger girls who were studying biology for their O-level examination at 16. I moved on to other schools and still had the same question. I continued to ponder this issue and took another job in a primary school (5–11 years) where I taught all subjects and introduced science. Subsequently, teaching only maths and science in a multicultural middle school helped me to understand how children interpreted their world, as did advising for a local education authority and running the education programme at the Zoological Society of London. After becoming an academic I continued to question this, and now I think I have found my answer. The realisation began when I had left teaching to have my own children. It was a revelation, watching my firstborn in particular, as he gradually noticed and made sense of his immediate world; as he began to ask questions and to explain it.

My answer: children establish the foundations of their knowledge and understanding in their home and their community, prior to their formal schooling. They observe and explain their causation, they also acquire names and other information from adults and the media, particularly from illustrated children's books and cartoons. The adults who care for them, usually mothers, are the first and most important teachers of the child. In some places around the world that role is also fulfilled by other relatives, or indeed by a whole community.

This book is written for practitioners and parents to help their children further develop their understanding of the living world from what they see and think about in the everyday. These emerging biologists do not have a curriculum to follow before they enter formal education, nor do adults have to comply with the demands of a formal statutory curriculum. Informal, pre-school learning is different; it is led by the learner and supported and facilitated by the adults.

Adults caring for emerging biologists are very important in children's lives. In these critical early years you spend a lot of time providing the child with experiences before they enter school. Everyday activities, such as dressing, washing up, playing together with a ball, observing the weather and cooking, are all examples of science in action, which includes mathematics, engineering and technology.

You are an expert at using these actions. Letting children carry them out is essential for their foundations of learning, especially in these important skills and practice. Don't let people tell you 'Oh play, it's a waste of time'. On the contrary, it is part of children's work and vital to their development in science, maths and technology. So encourage it.

Children learn biology and notice the effects of other sciences: physics, chemistry and Earth sciences, through observation and interpretation for themselves, giving rise to what is often pompously referred to as 'misconceptions'. These alternative conceptions are powerfully held, but careful teaching and instruction can move them towards a more scientific understanding. This is the role adults perform: observations and experiences may be incidental or planned, but again, the role of their first teachers, be they parents or carers, is crucial.

Children have a repository of biological knowledge and interpretation from their earliest years, often acquired through their personal, and directed, observations and experiences. Once they understand language they begin to 'label' items, giving them names. This is the beginning of taxonomy. Such an acquisition leads into biodiversity understanding, as do the other areas in which they learn.

These are:

1. Recognising anatomical features, enabling them to categorise, in the beginning, often non-biological categories.
2. Learning about physiology, such as the correlation between drinking and excreting.
3. Behaviours, movement, nest building, courtship, defence, hunting.
4. Habitats leading to ecological understanding. For example, Josh, aged 7, knew that frogs lived in water because he had a garden pond. But he also knew that they could live on land but needed to remain wet. He found a froglet in the grass and was concerned it would dry out; he picked up the young animal in his cupped hands, placed it in a paved area and covered it with wet grass. He put up a barrier of stones around it to make a secure habitat but then changed his mind and said that they needed a house, so instead placed a cardboard box over it.
5. Adaptations. Anatomical and physiological features that enable animals and plants to live successfully in their habitat, for example, the long forelimbs of brachiates: Josh had seen gibbons moving in a zoo.
6. Welfare. Children appear to have an instinct to look after animals, relating an animal's needs to their own, as illustrated by Josh as he cared for the froglet.

The chapters in this book follow young children's interests from themselves through to other animals and plants, changes, naming, Earth science and physical science.

Chapter 1 is about ourselves. Chapter 2 is about other animals, both vertebrates and invertebrates. Children's ideas, understanding and interpretation are discussed in Chapter 3. Plants fascinate children, their responses and comments are the focus of Chapter 4. Chapter 5 is about obvious changes, in particular in young plants, baby animals and ourselves as we grow up. This includes how living things, including plants, produce their offspring and how babies are cared for by the parent before and after birth until they are old enough to look after themselves, obtain food for themselves, as well as adapt to changes in the environment and respond to other living things. In Chapter 6 I discuss how children learn names, while Chapter 7 discusses the importance of Earth science: landscape and various different areas like forest and grassland, as well as the role of the planet in creating our climate on the Earth. The final chapter (Chapter 8), considers some basic aspects of the physical world, such as forces in living things.

 Talk science and activity boxes

Alongside key information about research, scientific concepts and ideas, each chapter contains suggested activities and discussion points. These activities are designed to encourage discussions, engagement and child-led investigations. Some of these may be more suitable for older learners or more experienced ones than those who are attending pre-school, but all activities can be modified to suit you and your child!

Very young children will not necessarily manage to carry out these activities in the same way as older children – something I have learnt from working on the same activity with both two-year-olds and four-year-olds – so see how your emergent biologists respond. The method outlined in this book may not be the best way for your children to tackle the activity. As educators we seek to encourage active learning and allow our intuitive scientists to ask questions. Try to design solutions which may or may not satisfy their questions, so that in re-designing those solutions you will encourage the child to rethink and try again. We do not tell them what to do, nor do we provide detailed information – that comes later in the formal school setting. Instead, we are trying to encourage them to think and wonder and work on their own initiative, rather than be dictated to by us.

Emergent biologists, as in any science, need to have informed ideas and exercise their imaginations in answering their questions. This is a very important aspect of being a scientist and, indeed, it is how research scientists actually work. They try again and again until they achieve a meaningful result. Or they may choose not to try again, remembering their first attempts at a later time and then changing what they did before. I hope the activities I have suggested assist you in developing foundations of sound scientific practice and aid you in teaching emergent biologists about our biological world.

Chapter 1

Beginning to learn about the living world

Introduction

Science is our everyday world. Our planet as we know it was created through Earth science, which has formed our landscapes and flora appropriate to the climates and soils in which animal life, including we, as humans, ultimately evolved. Living things 'obey' the laws of physics and are also composed of chemicals. Hence, all science is inter-linked. This book focuses on young children's learning of biological aspects of our living world, but also considers the influence of other sciences.

Types of knowledge

Education is concerned with gaining knowledge in our society. Children, like adults, gain much of their knowledge by direct observation and experience. As such, it is often referred to as 'conceptual', or factual and ideas knowledge. 'Procedural knowledge', on the other hand, is learnt from other people, such as young children, parents and carers, and other adults with whom children come into contact with at child care, nursery and play groups, as well as in the formal school setting when the child is older. Some aspects are learnt by children through trying things out – hands on activities are frequently called 'practice' or 'skills of science'. Linked with this acquisition is self-regulation and 'attitudinal knowledge', and awareness of perseverance and application at tasks and events. Both conceptual and procedural knowledge are also acquired through various forms of media. This is sometimes referred to as 'testimonial knowledge'. Intuition and the use of our existing knowledge are called 'inferential knowledge', and are often applied in children's investigations, decisions and problem solving.

Play – children's work

We have long known that play is crucial to child development (Moyles, 1989), and that society should promote awareness of this and work to change incorrect assumptions about play. Whitebread et al. (2012) point out that play is the work of children and is essential for intellectual achievement and emotional wellbeing.

Learning through experience is developed through both spontaneous and directed play, and the introduction of inquiry-based science fits well into extended play activities, progressing to problem-solving challenges. Play is, after all, largely concerned with problem solving (Moyles, 1989). 'Just playing' is a phrase that has been used in a derogatory sense by educators, and some parents and other adults, especially those who are unfamiliar with early years learners. Parents, perhaps reflecting on their own education, may assume a negative approach to play and fail to understand its essential and critical value.

Children play from their earliest years – play is how they learn and, initially, many play alone. However, learning is sometimes socially constructed whereby another form of cooperation is required or something has interested another child or an adult. Pretence and make-believe are essential and important aspects of play in a child's life.

In the development of play children often copy adult behaviours as they learn to separate objects and actions from the real world. They make new interpretations, thereby hypothesising and developing their thinking through imaginative and representational play. If actions are necessary when solving problems, the child gradually learns to work it out in their head, for example, they may use tangible tools and equipment in helping them to learn numeracy, for example matching pairs of blocks or leaves, or recognising different shapes of the same coloured blocks or flowers, or learning spatial words to describe where a certain part of a plant is found.

Spontaneous, free choice and unstructured play is important. Some play is representational with children imitating adult's behaviours, such as playing in the toy kitchen and making a pretend meal, going through all the actions they have observed. Mimicking in play activities they have seen also brings further learning experiences. Playing at childcare or even at home in a garden, in a mud kitchen, has two functions. It replicates actions they remember seeing elsewhere and also explores the properties of materials, for example mud. They often discover that familiar actions like pouring and stirring can prove to be a different task than that expected according to the material.

Today there is an emphasis on interactive learning as well as sociocultural aspects of learning. Dialogic talk (Alexander, 2008) is encouraged, rather than what might be called a didactic or declarative approach, that is to say, talking facts at learners. Fleer (1992) reminds us that constructivism places importance on determining learners' existing ideas. Hands-on activities are essential in the learning of science in the early years – scientific explanation does not need to be given, but practical experience of the phenomenon is essential to further learning. At this age, the foundations for observational and planning skills are laid down as well as the process skills such as manipulating items, collection and evaluation. Later on, in a child's formal science education, these fundamental experiences provide them with an experiential foundation on which to construct the necessary requirement of the curriculum. Children, from their earliest consciousness, observe and investigate. They play. In fact, they need to play (Moyles, 1989). Play can be referred to as messing about, in this case using 'science actions' in their play (Their and Linn, 1976).

You might observe young children before they express their thoughts out loud. These emergent, intuitive scientists have hidden questions which guide subsequent activities when further investigating. For example, a baby in a high chair drops something on the floor and observes what happens. In doing so the baby is collecting data through observation, where, very often, someone will return the object to them and they can then repeat the investigation.

Is playing a waste of time? Or is it an essential apprenticeship in developing scientific literacy? Children are often observed during play, which is divisible into experimental investigative play – when they explore phenomena – and narratives – when they are working through a past experience imaginatively or interpreting a story they have heard.

> Science, during early childhood, is it more than play? It is serious business. If we fail our children and students in science, the reasons may include lack of appropriate experiences during early childhood.
>
> (Roth, Goulart and Plakitsi, 2013)

Biological knowledge

Early years children achieve their understanding of the world using aspects of all categories of knowledge, as well as learning about themselves as biological beings – from being alive and by feeling hungry for instance. This I would term 'personal biological knowledge', and is an important aspect of how we experience our everyday world. We are all members of the biological domain and have personal experiences of being alive, which we extrapolate to other living things in our explanations about them. These explanations and descriptions, known as anthropomorphic comments, are used by children to interpret behaviours and appearances. I have concluded, as have other biologists, for example Ergazaki (2018), that young children have reasoning devices by which they are able to predict aspects of structure and behaviour in other living organisms using what they know about humans from themselves.

Becoming an emergent biologist

In focusing on how very young children acquire biological knowledge in the world around them, and thus become emergent biologists, the basic principles of the scientific processes of observation, classification and inquiry, hypothesis and prediction are used. The logistics of investigating, which is often called planning, include choosing the appropriate items and tools to use for the investigation, and is identifiable in the actions of the youngest child. Having an action plan is crucial and an important life skill. Being able to collect various sorts of data and to say what it means is another desirable skill, as is being able to communicate in different ways, particularly about outcomes and meaning. Acquiring the ability to share, collaborate and work as a team, are crucial aspects of 'doing' science, just as there are other aspects of playing and learning. Some are developmental and emerge as a young child grows older, usually at formal school where they can demonstrate this and apply it to other information, particularly to concepts and skills of accepted science. Thus, numeracy and literacy, language and communication, reading and talking are essential tools when learning the concepts and skills of science.

Intuitive scientists

Children are intuitive scientists from birth. The manifestation of science in our world shapes our reality and science has contributed to the technology with which our constructed world largely works (Gopnik, 2009). Like young children, scientists are curious and curiosity is central to discovery – investigating something because they want to know has led to all significant scientific knowledge and progress.

Many have observed, as reinforced by Agar (2017), that entry into a formal school system represses the natural curiosity of young children. Gopnik (2009) found through her work as a psychologist that young children were natural scientists. Tough (1977) listened to pre-school children's conversations at home in which they were always asking questions. Following the children through school, she found that the questions stopped. The children did not initiate questions, these were instead initiated by the teachers; the child was required to answer and the teacher closed the conversation with a comment, a classic teaching triadic dialogue. However, the work of Tizard and Hughes (1984) found that it was the school setting that also affected the young child's active questioning. Following the same children from home to school, they found the subsequent lack of questioning of some children depended on how comfortable they felt in school. It is known that young children, once they can speak at around two-and-a-half years of age, start asking questions all the time (British Association Early Childhood Education, 2012, p. 20).

Young children can justify, give reasons, share ideas and hypothesise a rationale for their ideas and actions. This approach is similar to that now advocated in much science teaching, a change from the teacher telling learners facts to learners making investigations, using an inquiry approach and justifying and thinking of the stages involved – a process known as argumentation. Young children often develop this approach spontaneously, but many practitioners are wary of using it (Erduran, Ozedem and Park, 2015).

Questioning

As educators, many of us have also recognised this use of questioning by children once they are in school. The school system seeks to encourage the development of knowledge and skills that are requirements of the statutory curriculum. However, skills advocated for early years children are also skills which are deemed necessary in science learning, hence, achieving one skill means that you achieve all of them, as these skills are easily transferable.

Children are natural storytellers. If you ask a simple question they often reply with a narrative. In science education, this construction of narratives links with a way of talking called argumentation. Essentially, it is the justification of decisions. Although, on occasion, the child will justify their action or identification with a reason, more often the action of an accompanying adult will encourage, through appropriate questions, the development of their child's thinking. For example, on seeing a different kind of animal for the first time a child is likely to say, for example, that it is a bird. You can ask him why does he think that it is a bird? Usually a child will identify the salient feature of a bird's behaviour: they notice that the animal is flying. Or children may deem the organism to be a bird because it has feathers, a feature seen in no other animal. Children will name things by recognising their shape and colour from memory, particularly books and animated cartoons they have seen in the media. One day, during one zoo visit, I heard a family deciding that the antelope at which they were looking was in fact a goat because the animal possessed goat characteristics of horns and hooves and explained this to the young children who were with them.

When a child notices organisms, perhaps a plant or animal that piques their interest, if they cannot name it you could ask them what they *think* it is? What does the organism look like, what does it resemble? What features or behaviours make them think that? In these instances children think 'what would happen if …?' and proceed with that action.

Ask children what happens when a stone is lifted from a green patch of grass, revealing a yellow patch instead. Why is it yellow, not green? What do they think has happened? Ask probing questions, 'What is the green grass having that the grass under the stone doesn't have?' Ask them to find out if that always happened and what they could do to test their ideas. Argumentation has become one of the key aspects of science in formal schooling but beginning with a child's justifying statements is an excellent start.

Narratives

Narratives are a key aspect of early years education. Pictorial books may use science that is fanciful; it may be accurate but most often it is a blend of both fact and fiction, depending on the story. A science-based narrative is part of the literary narrative which children quickly learn to identify. 'Doing' science also creates a narrative, which the child constructs for themselves in their early years and participates in at a later stage when the investigation is in a defined topic area. Langer (1953, p. 261) regarded narratives as an organisation device that allows the child (and adult) to organise their thoughts and experiences in a particular order. Bruner (1986) regarded this ordering, story sequencing, as a fundamental way of thinking. Very young children conduct a hidden narrative, which is revealed to us through their actions, but not verbalised. An early concept of possibility thinking was identified in sustained oral activity, which we might call a science exploration, or, there is mutuality and exchange between the child's imagination – their own created narratives and the questions they asked were prompted by their imagination (Cremin, Chappell and Craft, 2013). This is the case in learning and doing science in the early years.

Talk science

It is increasingly evident that children who have talked about science in their early years with family and friends, and carers and playgroup adults, are more likely to develop a lasting interest in, and take up, STEM (Science, Technology, Engineering and Maths) careers.

One of the most important things that we as adults might do for these emergent biologists is talk to them. Not to instruct, unless these youngsters are about to take a dangerous course of action, but instead to ask them questions, preferably divergent or open ones so they can compose their answer. However, on occasions a convergent or closed question is important such as, 'Can you see that bird over there?' Of course, the child may use the open mode of questioning to you. Even the ostensive remark out loud, 'Look at that!', which may direct their attention to something which you think of as interesting and/or important for them to see.

As well as discourse on children's responses to phenomena in the living world, this book is about children's interpretations of the living world, their own experience and understanding of phenomena. Often, these interpretations do not match the adult's understanding but may be misconceptions. For these young learners, however, they are alternative conceptions, or rather, the child's science, which will gradually change as they learn more. Their initial ideas are their explanations of what they see interpreted from what they know so far.

Cross-subject skills

Science educators expect young children to acquire links to developmental learning across communications, maths and technology. Early years documents do not make this point, but young learners are encouraged to master the connections through their developing understanding of the everyday world, which is science. Although this book focuses on the emergence of the child's biological understanding, these skills apply across all the sciences, which children do not recognise. They simply learn about their world.

Drawings

From the earliest times, cave drawings have been used by our species to record events such as hunts or the night sky. Drawings are constructed for a variety of purposes in science education. They are particularly pertinent in biological learning as 2D representations derived from the observation of organisms, external or internal structures (Tunnicliffe and Liston, 2002), or the drawing of the outline of a process (Tunnicliffe, 2004). A drawing, whatever it may look like to others, is a way that the child may choose to represent the inner mind (Cox, 1992, p. 88). Young children start by making marks on some paper, which then progresses to scribbling. They practice colouring in outlines and gradually learn to gain more control so the 'scribble' colouring stays more within that outline.

A number of researchers have described the stages in the development of drawing as the child develops his/her skill in creating an image that *most* resembles that which he/she is drawing. There are three stages in the development of children's drawings – a scribbling phase, followed by scribble symbolism and culminating in visual realisms, which have been described by Symington et al. (1981). Visual realism is said to develop between the ages of 8 to 12 years (Luquet, 1927, cited by Krampen, 1991).

Learning environment and the emerging scientific process

An adult working with a child, or a group of children, can create a learning environment in which science-learning experiences and opportunities can be developed and acquired through toys, play and observations of the everyday world. At the same time, it is possible to recognise and encourage intuitive science behaviour by observing what they find of interest, their body language, by listening to their spoken observations, comments, questions and ideas. In some cases they will try to answer for themselves as they question and justify their conclusions based on what they already know. You can assist them in this process by asking further questions and by offering your own answers.

Methods of observation and record keeping are essential in recording the progress of early years children. This will be expected by many parents or carers who also like to keep progress records of their child's learning. Whatever system you use, be it photographs, sticky notes or observation record sheets, you should be prepared to record systematically what is expected of you. Keeping up-to-date record sheets will enable you to:

- Observe actions, organisms and physical events.
- Interpret what they notice from their existing knowledge.

A guidelist

Do they:

> Hypothesise.
> Predict.
> Raise questions.
> Plan their investigations, explaining what they are doing and why.
> Choose what to do and what to use with justification – saying why they need to use these things.
> Collect data.
> Record data. Saying, drawing what happened is an early stage of data and evidence.
>
> (Monteira and Jiménez-Aleixandre, 2015)

My observations show that the following actions happen. They:

> Find patterns, matching, counting numbers, collecting items, for example, stones, leaves, pine cones. Same shape but different, for example.
> Evaluate outcomes – 'this happened', 'I thought it would', 'I didn't think it would'.
> Group items.
> Plan an investigation – 'I wonder what would happen if ...'
> Do what they think, using appropriate instruments (project management).
> Collaborate and share.
> Work out what they have found out.
> Communicate using a variety of ways that which he/she has done and found out.
> Name things using words they already know.
> Describe what they see and do within the limits of their vocabulary.
> Make up a word to describe what they are doing if they do not have the appropriate vocabulary.
> Learn new words from an adult.
> Explain by gestures and actions when they do not yet speak or only have a 'foreign' language in their learning situation with someone who does not speak it.

Photo journals

Start a photo journal of your children's science activities (Katz, 2012) and record biological phenomena which attract them, such as the year in a life of a deciduous tree. Children must all learn, for example as my eldest grandson did, that apples are not found on the apple tree all year round and at Christmas time the tree is bare. He was perplexed as he had noticed an apple in the preceding summer. However, when he came at Easter the following year it was in blossom and the following summer it once again had apples. Such a tangible record is a very useful one, which can be reflected upon and talked about with the child. It can be shared with their family members and, similarly, you can all share the child's home records at home when they are with you during the day.

Aspects of biology, the big ideas

Biology is about organising the living world into related categories.

It is also considered a basic human need to have a name for something. So, in the early years, notice what and how children allocate names to things and what criteria they use to do so. This relates to the grouping of items and the collections they make as well as living organisms and actions.

Be aware of the big ideas in biology they may notice, for example, that animals do not move by themselves or that most animals can have different body coverings. There are animals, such as cats, with four legs on the ground and others, like birds, that have only two legs but also wings. All plants have some green to their appearance and have roots which fix them in the soil, yet not all plants have flowers.

Accept their explanations but, when appropriate, show and explain what we know using the correct terminology, for example, not 'disappear' but instead 'dissolve'. Use the term 'mammals' for four-legged animals and don't assume that all plants have flowers – avoid using stereotypical terms such as 'daisy-like flowers'; bear in mind that trees are also flowering plants in the same way that smaller species fall into the same category.

Asking the children questions

The young child continually questions things and we can encourage their understanding and further development by asking our own questions. Use terms such as 'What would happen if ...?', 'Could you ...?', rather than instructing them to do something, unless, of course, their intended action is dangerous. We have to judge what is appropriate, but children should be encouraged to assess a risk for themselves. While we mostly focus on 'open' questions, 'closed' or convergent questions require a definitive answer, for example, 'Can you see that stone on the ground?' Yes or no is the answer anticipated. Such questions are used in some teaching as a way of checking if the learner actually learnt something in the lesson! This method belongs to the classic triadic dialogue formula (Scott, 2008) and is rarely employed now. In the triadic dialogue, the teacher initiates as follows: teacher asks question, child answers, teacher closes the dialogue. In my work in education in zoos I noticed that a reverse triadic dialogue was heard more often from children (Patrick and Tunnicliffe, 2012, p. 95). The child asked a question, such as 'What is that?', pointing at an unfamiliar animal, the adult replied, usually with an everyday name, and the child made a comment and closed that short discourse, moving on to another observation or animal.

Maths and biology

Shape, space and measure, and basic numeracy are integral to talking and doing science. Sometime a closed question is appropriate, for example, 'How many cars do you have there?', and we should respond with 'And count ... one, two, three cars!'. Children need to hear words and syntax in action so that they can learn, and this is just as important in the learning of science as it is elsewhere in the formal curriculum. In biology, children observe shapes and spaces and use words to describe the basic shape of an animal or a leaf. They distinguish, sometimes in relative sizes, between a large fruit and small one for instance, using the appropriate language of 'big', 'smaller' and so on. Similarly, they can describe shapes, such as 'My cat has a rectangular body, but his ears are triangular'. This is maths in everyday action and should be encouraged.

Conclusion

The key action with early learners is to encourage experiences while focusing on their own observations and interactions in everyday life. For example, how they experience the phenomena of landscape, climate and organisms in their particular environment while encouraging them to talk about what they see. To learn names of actions, objects and organisms; to be able to ask questions and receive appropriate information; to be encouraged to develop those observations, explanations and questions, expanding and using the new vocabulary as it is heard. At first, children focus on themselves and the closest humans to them – the next chapter considers what they learn when they focus on themselves.

References

Agar, J. (2017) *The Curious History of Curiosity Driven Research*. 2016 Wilkins-Bernal-Medawar Lecture. London: The Royal Society, 4 April 2017. Available at: https://royalsociety.org/search/?query=the%20curious.

Alexander, R. (2008) *Towards Dialogic Teaching: Rethinking Classroom Talk*. Cambridge: Dialogos. York.

Bruner, J. (1986) *Actual Minds, Possible Worlds*. Cambridge, MA: Harvard University Press.

Cox, M. (1992) *Children's Drawings*. London: Penguin.

Cremin, T., Chappell, K. and Craft, A. (2013) Reciprocity between narrative, questioning and imagination in the early and primary years: examining the role of narrative in possibility thinking. *Thinking Skills and Creativity*, 9: 135–151.

Erduran, S., Ozedem, Y. and Park, J.-Y. (2015) Research trends on argumentation in science education. A journal content analysis from 1998–2014. *International Journal of STEM Education*, 2(5): 1–12.

Ergazaki, M. (2018) Biology and young children. In Kampourakis, K. and Reiss, M.J. (eds), *Teaching Biology in Schools: Global Research, Issues, and Trends*. Abingdon, UK: Routledge, pp. 22–34.

Fleer, M. (1992) Identifying teacher-child interaction which scaffolds scientific thinking in young children. *Science Education*, 76(4): 373–397.

Gopnik, A. (2009) *The Philosophical Baby: What Children's Minds Tell Us about Truth, Love, and the Meaning of Life*. London: The Bodley Head.

Katz, P. (2012) Using photo books to encourage young children's science identities. *Journal of Emergent Science*, 3(Spring–Summer): 25–31.

Krampen, M. (1991) *Children's Drawings: Iconic Coding of the Environment*. New York: Plenum Press.

Langer, S.K. (1953) *Feeling and Form*. London: Routledge & Kegan Paul.

Luquet, G.H. (2001[1927]) *Le Dessin Enfantin* [Children's Drawings], trans. A. Costall. London: Free Association Books.

Monteira, S.F. and Jiménez-Aleixandre, M.P. (2015) The practice of using evidence in kindergarten: the role of purposeful observation. *Journal of Research in Science Teaching*, 5(8): 1232–1258.

Moyles, J.R. (1989) *Just Playing? The Role and Status of Play in Early Childhood Education*. Milton Keynes, UK: Open University Press.

Roth, W.-M., Goulart, M.I.M. and Plakitsi, K. (2013) *Science Education in Early Childhood: A Cultural-Historical Perspective*. Cultural Studies of Science Education 6. Dordrecth: Springer.

Scott, P. (2008) Talking a way to understanding in science classrooms. In Mercer, N. and Hodgkinson, S. (eds), *Exploring Talk in Schools*. London: Sage Publications, pp. 17–36.

Symington, D., Boundy, K., Radford, T. and Walton, J. (1981) Children's drawings of natural phenomena. *Research in Science Education*, 11(1): 44–51.

The British association for early childhood education. (2012) *The Early Years Foundation Stage Development Matters*. [online] Foundation Years. Available at: http://www.google.co.uk/url?sa=t&rct=j&q=&esrc=s&source=web&cd=2&ved=0CCYQFjAB&url=http%3A%2F%2Fwww.foundationyears.org.uk%2Ffiles%2F2012%2F03%2FDevelopment-Matters-FINAL=PRINT-

Their, H. and Linn, M.N. (1976) The value of interactive learning experiences. *Curator*, 19(3): 233–242.

Tizard, B. and Hughes, M. (1984) *Young Children Learn: Talking and Thinking at Home and School*. London: Fontana.

Tough, J. (1977) *The Development of Meaning*. London: George Allen & Unwin.

Tunnicliffe, S.D. (2004) Where does the drink go? *Primary Science Review*, 85(November–December): 8–10.

Tunnicliffe, S.D. and Litson, S. (2002) Observation or imagination? *Primary Science Review*, 71: 25–27.

Whitebread, D., Basilio, M., Kuvalja, M. and Verma, M. (2012) *The Importance of Play: A Report on the Value of Children's Play with a Series of Policy Recommendations*. Brussels, Belgium: Toys Industries for Europe.

Chapter 2

Learning about ourselves

Introduction

In scientific terms, we are members of the species *Homo sapiens*, belonging to the family *Hominidae*, which includes apes. Although the coccyx at the end of the spinal column remains, humans are, in fact, tail-less primates. Children being natural observers and inquirers of the world around them learn from first-hand experiences related to themselves, and they acquire knowledge of their own and other people's bodies through interactions in the community and culture in which they live. This experience and knowledge, therefore, is not necessarily gained from formal education within the classroom (Tunnicliffe and Reiss, 1999; Reiss and Tunnicliffe, 2001).

External features of the body

One of the earliest activities carers introduce to babies is the naming of external parts of their bodies. These activities are often associated with various rhymes, through which they also learn the rhythm of their first language. Babies learn as they encounter various external parts of their own bodies and those of others, particularly their mother.

Children hear references to parts of the body, internal and external. For instance, people say 'stomach' or 'tummy', and rub over its internal location or touch the child's head and say 'use your brain'. They can point to an external part if asked, even before they can speak. We observed that when asked to put a small card featuring an external body part, for example, a nose, a foot, a head or an ear, on a cut-out of a child's shape, very young two-year-old children took great delight in placing the card on the actual named part of the body. Older children in this pre-school group placed the cards on the picture. After this inclination emerged we made a sticky note with the name of the part written on it, and gave it to the child when we had shown them the picture card. The sticky notes proved an interactive, fun and effective way of teaching early learners to name body parts. Young children took great delight in walking around as a 'sticky-note' person.

Children also hear references to some parts of the body through daily life instructions. They begin to associate requests such as 'please wash your hands' with that body part before they can speak. One of my grandsons, when he was 4 years old, kept drawing himself (Figure 2.1). I have many copies of these drawings, all similar. He could not explain the symbol 'M', which he had included on his drawings. This drawing is typical of young children, the 'tadpole man'. We have found similar drawings in many parts of the world, irrespective of language and culture. The development of a child's drawing skill is discussed

Learning about ourselves   15

Figure 2.1 Tadpole man drawn by a 4-year-old boy

in Chapter 1 (page 19) but, essentially, they start with marks on paper, or elsewhere, such as walls. They enjoy making marks and controlling the crayon or whatever implement they pick up. Development through these stages has been described by various researchers, e.g. Symington et al. (1981).

Figure 2.1 shows the very basic shape used to represent a human and often drawn by young children.

 Talk science: drawing

What do they like to draw?
When and what do they like to use?
Pencil, crayon? On paper?
Do they have a drawing programme on a tablet?

 Activity: what can you draw?

Encourage your child to draw things other than themselves, for example, their pet or their house. The use of small white boards is very useful but you cannot document the image so try photographing it instead.

16 Learning about ourselves

As they develop children are beginning to differentiate the parts of the human body but at first, they draw blob heads with stick legs. As they develop further, they begin to draw more accurate proportions with tubes as appendages.

 Talk science: naming parts of the body

Ask your child what the different, outside parts of his/her body are called.
Sing a song together such as 'Fingers and Toes'.
Count how many of each part you have, e.g. how many feet, toes on a foot; altogether how many toes do you have between you?
Can your child point to the same parts of a human body on you?
Can they name the similar parts on a pet?

 Activity: naming yourself

Download labels for different body parts from the internet, or make your own. Write the name of those external parts on a note. Ask the child to label an outline of a body. You can draw an outline of the child, perhaps using a volunteer! When we have done this, we find the youngest children delight in sticking a name label on themselves and have great fun. Once they can label their own structure can they think about it and label a doll for major parts like arms. Using a picture or a soft toy, ask them to label parts with sticky notes – this is more difficult.

Inside the body

Drawings are a universal form of communication; free of linguistic variation, they transcend cultural and language barriers. Analysing drawings executed by children is one method of how we can learn about children's developing understanding of themselves, and other organisms (see Chapters 3 and 4), by eliciting an expressed model. With other colleagues, I have used drawings as a technique in establishing primary children's understanding of the internal organisation of a familiar vertebrate – themselves. Using a rubric, we analysed and scored our findings to identify a progression from a simple to a more complex understanding. This was first devised by Tunnicliffe and Reiss (1999), but the rubric has been adapted by other researchers, e.g. Prokop and Fančovičová (2006).

Using drawings is just one way of gathering information about children's understanding of scientific phenomena (White and Gunstone, 1992). It has been increasingly used to find what children think is inside themselves. One of the most thoroughly studied systems is the skeleton (Gellert, 1962; Caravita and Tonucci, 1987; Guichard, 1995; Cox, 1997; Tunnicliffe and Reiss, 1999), however, other systems have been studied too, such as the digestive system (Teixeira, 1998). Pre-secondary school children's understanding of linked systems have also been studied by the use of drawings. For example, Prokop, Fančovičová and Tunnicliffe (2009) studied the understanding of the urinogenital system and the endocrine system.

Biological awareness and interpretation are unlike other aspects in the world of a child, in which they are constructing their knowledge and interpreting the world on their own terms. A child is a part of the biological world, rather than simply an observer of it, as all humans are in the physical world.

The first body parts and functions of which a child becomes aware are its own. If the child is breast-fed, s/he develops an awareness of that particular part of their mother's body and its function. A toddler at a workshop was shown a table with an assortment of model animals on, and from these he chose a sheep and a lamb. He turned the model onto its back and put the lamb on its abdomen, with the instruction, 'feed'. His mother was with him and said he had been breast-fed until he was almost 2 years old. Children playing with dolls will imitate childcare and feeding, sometimes pretending to breastfeed or otherwise feed with a doll-sized bottle. Both boys and girls will wrap up the 'baby' and carefully, in a pushchair, imitate what they have seen adults doing.

We humans are like many other animals with which young children may be familiar, such as dogs and cats; we are animals with jaws and we have four limbs, in our case two arms and two legs. Each limb ends in five digits, which we teach children are called 'fingers and toes'. This makes us, like dogs, cats, dinosaurs, birds, fish and amphibians, four-limbed animals – tetrapods. Establishing the four-limbed structure helps develop numeracy as counting the many appendages of an animal is a useful and fun way of consolidating number practice, involving basic biology as well as numeracy and science observation skills. Very young children can still move their toes in a way similar to other primates, such as chimps, which are, in evolutionary terms, our nearest relatives. When children visit zoos, and to a lesser extent natural history museums, they are fascinated by the resemblance of animals or fibreglass models of animals, to themselves (see Chapter 4).

While often intrigued, these early learners may be puzzled without an external body similar to humans, which the child has to put together to form a human body. Alternatively, having pictures of external parts and asking the child to show where they are on an outline of a child helps them learn both the positions and names of parts.

We can explore their mental models through analysing the expressed model (Gilbert, Boulter and Elmer, 2000), as visible in their drawings. The study reported here employed an analysis of the children's drawings, which were then used as the probe for an interview with each child, explaining the expressed model and its role in an interview where the child was invited to talk about each organ they had drawn. The researcher (Tunnicliffe) pointed to each part of the drawing in turn, from the head down, asking what the part they had drawn represented, what it did, where they had found out about it and if there was anything else they wished to explain. Extending the question, the responses were then recorded. The children were then asked to talk about what else they knew but had not drawn, and if they could say why they had not drawn it. This represents the probed drawing technique. Finally, the words as probes to drawings were carried out with the same class as they developed. Of the original class, at the beginning of school, only seven of the original children remained at the end of their time in primary school. The town was in the home counties of England, within daily travelling distance to London and was therefore a very mobile community.

18   Learning about ourselves

How we discovered the children's ideas

On each visit to the class, at the same time in the Spring Term, each child was asked to do a drawing on A4 paper of 'What is inside you'. Each child was subsequently interviewed individually about their drawing at the side of the class area. I pointed to each item of the drawing, using the drawing as a probe for further information such as what it was, what it did and how they had learnt about it. Drawings were scored using a previously validated and published scoring system which emphasises biological understanding and minimises the importance of drawing ability.

The analysis criteria used is given in Tables 2.1 and 2.2 (Reiss and Tunnicliffe, 2001).

Table 2.1 Analysis criteria for the presence of organs

Level and definition of vertebrate skeletal system

Level 1	No representation of internal structure.
Level 2	One or more internal organs (e.g. bones and blood) placed at random.
Level 3	One internal organ (e.g. brain or heart) in appropriate position.
Level 4	Two or more internal organs (e.g. stomach and a bone 'unit' such as the ribs) in appropriate positions but no extensive relationships indicated between them.
Level 5	One organ system indicated (e.g. gut connecting head to anus)
Level 6	Two or three major organ systems indicated out of skeletal, gaseous exchange, nervous, digestive, endocrine, urinogenital, muscular and circulatory.
Level 7	Comprehensive representation with four or more organ systems indicated out of skeletal, gaseous exchange, nervous, digestive, endocrine, urinogenital, muscular and circulatory.

Reiss and Tunnicliffe (2001)

Table 2.2 Definition criteria for organ systems

System and definition

Skeletal system	Skull, spine, ribs and limbs.
Gaseous exchange system	Two lungs, two bronchi, windpipe which joins to mouth and/or nose.
Nervous system	Brain, spinal cord, some peripheral nerve (e.g. optic nerve).
Digestive system	Through tube from mouth to anus and indication of convolutions and/or compartmentalisation.
Endocrine system	Two endocrine organs (e.g. thyroid, adrenals, pituitary) other than pancreas [scored within digestive system] or gonads [scored within urinogenital system].
Urinogenital system	Two kidneys, two ureters, bladder and urethra *or* two ovaries, two fallopian tubes and uterus *or* two testes, two epididymes and penis.
Muscular system	Two muscle groups (e.g. lower arm and thigh) with attached points of origin.
Circulatory system	Heart, arteries and veins into and/or leaving heart and, at least to some extent, all round the body.

Reiss and Tunnicliffe (2001)

This scoring system (also used in Tunnicliffe and Reiss, 1999) requires a definition of organ systems. The eight organ systems (which are also used in Reiss and Tunnicliffe, 2001) were as in Table 2.2.

The collected drawings were analysed for content using the rubric of Tunnicliffe and Reiss (1999). In the analyses (Tables 2.3 and 2.4), the small letter of the organ system to which the organ belonged indicates an organ, whereas the capital letter represents the drawing of a whole system. For instance, if a bone was indicated it was scored an 's' for a component of the skeletal system, but if a representation of a whole skeleton with pelvis and pectoral girdles, limbs, ribs and skull together with vertebrate column were drawn it was denoted as an 'S'.

Girl 2 was present throughout all the years, from the start of primary school to the end but, unfortunately, had a special lesson during the drawing session, so could not participate. Such is school life.

The interviews were interesting. Several times I heard phrases such as, 'If you didn't have bone you'd be jelly on the floor', and that blood was made in thigh bones. Further probing revealed this is what they had been told in Year 4 (8 years old), when the then National Curriculum specified, remarking about the human body, 'Our teacher (named) told in Year 4', was the noted influence of teacher, Year 4.

From this work it emerged that the development of understanding is a) awareness of organs; b) name of organ; c) position of organ (approximately); d) function of organs, e.g. 'brain for thinking'; e) multiple functions; and f) interrelationships, systems.

What we found out

Drawings show a lack of a holistic interrelationship overall, although a few are beginning to show such understanding. For example, at Year 4, Boy 4 drew a skeletal and digestive system. At Year 6 he repeated the drawing of a skeletal system but was only scored Level 5 for his drawing because he only indicated one item; in his Year 5 interview he described the skeletal system and the urogenital system. This was difficult, so he did no drawing with a body outline, but separate organs, thus not indicating any system. However, in Year 6 he only indicated by drawing the skeletal system and a urogenital organ. He drew a muscle, as did Boys 1, 3 and 5 and Girl 1. Boy 1,

Table 2.3 A summary of the levels, organs and systems obtained by the children

Level	Organs (see protocol for key)	Systems
Level 6 = 3	n = 12	D = 3
Level 5 = 2	g = 18	C = 2
Level 4 = 17	c = 18	G = 1
	d = 19	
	s = 1	
	m = 8	
	u = 8	
	e = 3	

Table 2.4 Summary of scores from drawing a kidney by the seven children who were still at this school at the end of their primary education. The organ is denoted by the small letter of the system to which it belongs. The system is indicated by the capital letter

Name	Yr 1	Yr 2	Yr 3	Yr 4	Yr 5	Yr 6	Notes
	5–6 yrs	6–7 yrs	7–8 yrs	8–9 yrs	9–10 yrs	10–11 yrs	
Boys							
B1	4 sdc	4ncs	absent	4ncds	4 nsd	4 ncrdums drawn outside body and position indicated by arrows.	Same level 4 but more organs and more sophisticated drawings as aged.
B2	3s Told a story – man with a dog etc.	4 scr	absent	absent	ncsu (No drawing) mentions pelvis and bladder.	4 nrcdus	Yr 1 bones in body – heart drawn in isolation; drew an army ship talked about blood; man with a dog and sword in stone and a snake.
B3	3 nsc	2 d Drew tongue and stomach in isolation.			6 NnCcSsm	4 from drawing crndsum BUT 6 from transcript RC	Transcript describes R and C. Drawings have organs drawn outside body outline and arrow to position – systems hence not shown but described.
B4	4 nsc	2 ncsr placed at random.		6 DdSsnucr	No drawing 6 SscrudUu from transcript.	5 nSsmcud 6 from transcript N	Lots of muscles as individual units. Strong school influence Yr 4. Hips drawn, shoulder blade, vertebrae (on Yr 5 transcript).
B5	Body + s Parts drawing 3(ribs) talk = 4 cdn.	4 csur		4 snrdc	4 snrdcu	ncdrmsmc Drawing level 2 organs at random.	Learnt Yr 1 at local science centre 'Lookout'. Read Yr 1 transcript tube in big square (+ large intestine) Yr 2 had been to Millennium Dome. Muscles appear Level 6, penis dripping sperm at Level 4.
Girls							
G1	3 ncs	4 ncs	absent	4mncs	4 nmcsr	4 nmcsrud Extensive bits but no organ systems. 5 R from transcript.	5 R from transcript drew liver, bladder, kidneys, described respiratory system. Yr 1 and 2 same organs n c s Yr 1 says brains, blood, bones but says Yr 2 heart pumps blood, brain is for thinking. Keen on face muscles, gives one organ and a function at 4, e.g. face muscles open mouth; ribs protect heart; bones hold you upright. Yr 3 brain is for thinking.
G2	2 s	4 ncs	away	4 ncsr	4 ncsrd 'the Alien'.	Not done, called out.	Voice box Yr 5, Yr 4 and 5 talks about funny bone, shoulder at Yr 4 (8 years old).

Table 2.5 A summary of organs and systems mentioned overall by the seven children

Name	Number organs n = 101	Systems n = 12
Nervous system nN	22	2
Skeletal sS	25	4
Digestive dD	13	1
Cardiac cC	23	2
Respiratory rR	13	2
Urinogenital uU	9	1
Muscular mM	7	0

Note: systems mentioned and explained, showing the systems were understood from the probed interviews but not indicated by drawings: three for N, one S, two R, two C, one D and one U. No child showed an understanding of the muscular system.

present every year, scored Level 4 at every class, he merely 'collected' organs. Such results indicate the limitation of using only one method of assessment.

Along with the knowledge of a few organs, such as bone and heart, children gradually learned more organs but few developed an understanding of a system, as defined in the rubric. All children had some awareness in Year 1 at Level 4. It was not uncommon among the whole class of the time to do so because they knew of two organs and their approximate position; the year where they were formally taught about the human body, subsequent years just added awareness of further organs, as illustrated by Boy 1.

Some organs were learnt about through personal experience. Girl 1 went from Level 3 in Year 1 to Level 4 in Year 2 but remained Level 4 'ncms' in Year 4, adding 'muscles' to her repertoire, and in Year 5 adding 'respiratory organs'. In Year 6 she added a digestive organ, the liver, which is complex, and which we had not included in our original rubric. She did not know its function and was scored a 'd'. Unlike Boys 4 and 5, she did not omit previous organs. Girl 1, unusually, drew a liver. Some pupils missed out organs at Year 6 that had been mentioned at Year 5 or lower (e.g. Boy 4's drawings in Year 4 were marked as Level 6 (S D), but in Year 6 were at Level 5 as he omitted parts and 'lost' D from Year 4). Muscles appear for Boy 4 at Year 6 but as individual units. No reproductive organs were drawn except for Boy 5 in Year 4 who drew a penis with drips of fluid, which he labelled sperm. However, external organs were not considered in this study. Some children in early years drew a head with hair, eyes and a mouth indicated, occasionally ears, revealing the desire for realism externally. But some children also indicated the brain as an internal organ.

 Talk science: inside you

Ask your child if they know what they have inside them? How do they know? Where have they found out about that?

> **Activity: label**
>
> Why not mark on a photo or drawing what they say when asked questions about their body parts. Date the entry and next time you talk about this mark their 'organ knowledge' on a new drawing. Do this over a period of time. You choose the time intervals. Keep these records to document their growing understanding.

Out of school learning

Children do not learn just in school. We as teachers do not know their exposure to information other than at home or during out-of-school visits. One child mentioned a local science centre and a museum of natural history displaying models of the human body with removable organs. Another mentioned television. One boy mentioned, in particular, his class teacher in Year 4!

Home was the main source of knowledge mentioned, particularly involving mothers, books and personal experience. Girl 2 described asthma because her friend had it and she showed an understanding of the respiratory system. She also mentioned the 'funny bone' from personal experience. Another boy knew about kidneys because his father was receiving dialysis. Girl 2, in Year 5, also talked about a collar bone (clavicle), but did not show any indication of the pectoral girdle, as she had heard someone had broken it; she also knew about lungs and the trachea, scoring R from her interview (because her friend had asthma). These children had a personal context to which they could relate their knowledge.

One organ, one function

Boy 2 began in Year 1 with a story about a man with a dog, a snake and a sword in a stone, but at Year 6 drew a traditional drawing with no story (organs n r c d u) and mentioned one organ/one function in his interview, for example, the windpipe helps you breathe. Interviewing children about their drawings reveals, unsurprisingly, a depth of understanding of functions not revealed through the drawings alone and thus gives a fuller picture of understanding. Several children knew about organs and their approximate position but not their specific function in an interview, for example, the liver, the bladder and kidneys – are these, therefore, the less 'popular' organs'?

So what did this tell us?

Level 4 in knowledge of internal anatomy is the most frequent level attained by students and adults (Reiss and Tunnicliffe, 2001). It appears that there is a comfort level at which humans in our society know enough to get by with – and there is, from anecdotal evidence, the same levelling-off in knowledge about phenomena and artefacts in many areas. A sufficiency, but not a *proficiency*, of knowledge is the norm. There appears from this and other work (for example Reiss and Tunnicliffe, 2001), to be a ranking of familiarity of organs. It begins with the brain, heart, stomach and bones in general, adding the lungs and the ribs as a unit and long bones of legs early on, eventually forming another bone unit.

Thus, over the six years of primary education, while there were periods of stasis, there was a tendency for children to know more about individual organ systems as they grew older. Some children entered school with Level 4 knowledge and left the primary school not having attained a higher level of knowledge, rather, they simply added to their list of organs. Such an increase might be because of particular teachers and particular teaching, which some pupils acknowledged. Other sources of knowledge include family members, books, television, personal experience and science museums/centres. Children have a misunderstanding that skeletons are joined to each other, but have no clear understanding of ligaments, nor of the relationship of bones to muscles. This is created, we think, by two factors: first, animated cartoons, where complete, often stylised skeletons are depicted running around; and, second, articulated skeletons on display in natural history museums.

How can we help children learn?

Perhaps teachers could be taught in training and by in-service development courses to teach from cell level, building up to organs and their interconnectedness with systems – a systems approach. Teaching functions holistically with interconnections of systems is more effective than teaching system by system because they all interact. Hence, the diaphragm is the muscle most often indicated on drawings of older pupils, which we suspect is because it is taught in senior schools along with the respiratory system. The classic drawing of a longitudinal section of the upper torso is the one studied and recalled, with the diaphragm as its lower boundary in post-primary school education. Children rarely draw a diagram in primary school; their indication of muscles is usually limited to knee muscles drawn within the outline of a limb and shown as unconnected to bones. Prospective parents are now, more usually, prepared in ways of helping their offspring to learn. So too are school learners in childcare, or other similar courses related to developing citizens.

Home, family and the wider community are rich sources of learning. Not all children have opportunities to explore museums and science centres. Be on the alert for children who are missing out, especially if you work with children identified as less advantaged. Whatever language you use, be aware of cultural and language differences.

Conclusion

Learning about ourselves is the first stage in beginning to understand the living world and the existence of other living things. Children use themselves as a template for explaining other living things but gradually realise that, while living things share the same needs, obtaining them is solved in different ways. Thus, the next chapter considers other living animals.

References

Caravita, S. and Tonucci, F. (1987) How children know biological structure-function relationships. Paper presented at the Second International Seminar: Misconceptions and Educational Strategies in Science and Mathematics, 26–29 July, Cornell University, Ithaca, NY.

Cox, M. (1997) *Drawings of People by the Under-5s*. London: Falmer Press.

Gellert, E. (1962) Children's conceptions of the content and functions of the human body. *Genetic Psychology Monographs*, 65: 293–405.

Gilbert, J.K., Boulter, C.J. and Elmer, R. (2000) Positioning models in science education and in design and technology. In Gilbert, J.K. and Boulter, C.J. (eds), *Developing Models in Science Education*. Dordrecht: Kluwer, pp. 3–17.

Guichard, J. (1995) Designing tools to develop the conception of learners. *International Journal of Science Education*, 17(2): 243–253.

Prokop, P. and Fančovičová, J. (2006) Students' ideas about the human body: do they really draw what they know? *Journal of Baltic Science Education*, 10: 86–95.

Prokop, P., Fančovičová, J. and Tunnicliffe, S.D. (2009) The effect of type of instruction on expression of children's knowledge: how do children see the endocrine and urinary system? *International Journal of Environmental and Science Education*, 4(1): 75–93.

Reiss, M.J. and Tunnicliffe, S.D. (2001) Students' understandings of human organs and organ systems. *Research in Science Education*, 31(3): 383–399.

Symington, D., Boundy, K., Radford, T. and Walton, J. (1981) Children's drawings of natural phenomena. *Research in Science Education*, 11(1): 44–51.

Teixeira, F.M. (1998, November) *What happens to the food we eat? Children's conceptions of the structure and function of the digestive system*. Paper presented at the Conference of European Researchers in Didaktik of Biology, University of Göteborg, Göteborg, Sweden.

Tunnicliffe, S.D. and Reiss, M.J. (1999) Student's understandings about animal skeletons. *International Journal of Science Education*, 21(11): 1187–1200.

White, R. and Gunstone, R. (1992) *Probing Understanding*. New York: The Falmer Press.

Chapter 3

Learning about other animals

Introduction

The term 'scientific literacy' is increasingly used to refer to the understanding of scientific concepts and processes, and is considered necessary for citizens to be capable of making decisions and evaluating evidence put to them regarding issues in society. Acquiring scientific literacy, together with developing literacy in terms of talking, listening, writing and reading, as well as numeracy, is a complex task for most early years pupils. This book is focused on biological literacy, which also develops from those earliest years; as children are biological beings they acquire an understanding of basic life functions from first-hand experience as well as a rudimentary understanding of the biological form and function of organisms in their relationship with the environment (Freeman and Bracegirdle, 1971; Ghazali and Tolmie, 2014). However, even in the first quarter of the 21st century, the situation has not improved since Tunnicliffe and Reiss (1999) stated that '... to date, insufficient work has been carried out on how children view living organisms in the environment'. Korfiatis and Tunnicliffe (2012) point out that a 2-year-old boy had five words for animals in his first 50 words and also that observing animals feeding, as well as observing what they do and where they live, is a frequent pastime of very young children. Thus, biology becomes part of a child's conceptual framework from their earliest years. Disappointingly, despite recognition by some educators of the critical age for learning biology (Tunnicliffe and Ueckert, 2011), the study of the relationship of living organisms to each other and their environment is only a small part of the school curriculum in most countries. Allen (2015), in eliciting taxonomic knowledge of pre-school children, found that they held naïve ideas, which were also found in older children. Disturbingly for biology educators, his research found that while some of the non-biological ideas disappeared as the children developed, other, inaccurate ideas began to emerge. His work also concluded that children learn about animals in a variety of places, formal and informal, as well as learning of their changes with maturation.

How children learn about other animals

As educators, we are interested in how children learn. Children have an inherent interest in natural objects, and animals are an important focus of that interest (Tomkins and Tunnicliffe, 2007). In some societies young children are given toy animals (usually that of a mammal) made of fabric, to which they can develop a great attachment, and they often recognise the real animal the soft toy represents even if the toy is rather unrealistic and stylised (Tunnicliffe et al., 2008). The movement of animals attracts even the youngest child; they may want to touch animals that come near them and, gradually, the child learns the successful way to interact. They are fascinated by animals and enjoy seeing various kinds – visits to zoos and animal parks encourage this fascination.

 Talk science: what is it?

What features help a child recognise birds for example? What reasons do they give if you ask? What is the difference between two birds that you see regularly, such as a pigeon and a robin? What names do your children have for their soft toys, which are based on animals? What animals do you know? Where have you seen them? What makes an animal an animal?

 Activity: where is it?

You need photographs, or the real animal! Ask the child to point out on a photograph where they consider something to be and why. Invite the child to draw an outline of the animal and insert organs. You can draw the outline for them to intrigue them if necessary!

It is important to provide carefully planned, supportive learning experiences for early years children in order to support their scientific development beyond basic emotional reactions to living organisms. This will lead to a deeper understanding of the living world beyond their human-centric one and allow them to move towards an interest in the issues of sustainability of the planet and conservation of organisms and their habitats.

Animals as symbols

Many countries are represented by a national animal or bird. For example, a lion (UK), an eagle (USA), a tiger (India), and so on. A useful activity with young children would be to identify as many countries as you can which have animals and birds as symbols.

 Activity: what am I?

Assemble a collection of plastic model animals, including both farm and zoo animals. Ask the child the name of each animal and what kind of animal it is. Can the child group several animals that they think belong together? (E.g. zoo animals or farm animals, males and females, mothers and babies.) Why do they make each grouping – ask what their reasons for these groupings are (are they all large or small perhaps? Are they the same colour?)

Places to live

See the discussion point and activity below which will help children think about the different habitats in which animals might live.

 Talk science: where do I live?

Where do you live? What is your place? Your town or village?
Do you know in which country you live? Do you know where this is in the world?
Do you know of any other counties near to you? Have you been to a country other than the one in which you live? Are there any other countries a long way from your country? Which animals do we see at home and near home? Do you know of any kinds of animals that do not normally live in our country?

 Activity: where do animals live?

This activity depends on a child understanding representations of maps.
Large floor mats printed with a world map can be used to introduce the names of countries and also identify where an animal comes from. You can look at pictures or videos of animals and identify where each animal chooses to live naturally.

Children around the world notice animals and plants

Patrick et al. (2013) looked at the knowledge children (aged 6, 10 and 15 years) have of animals from a cross-cultural perspective. Students from six countries (Brazil, England, Finland, Iceland, Portugal, USA) were asked to list as many animals as possible and state where they had seen or learned about the animals. The results were analysed and they indicated that first, these learners were aware of animals. Second, they are more aware of mammals as examples of those animals. The work confirmed that there is a globally shared, 'folk' biological knowledge of animals which children learned and that, third, children learned about animals during sociocultural interactions.

Learning from looking at real animals

Children learn much from directly observing animals in action and making sense of what they see at home and outside, for example on their way to school (Specktor-Levy et al. 2011) and in school. Children observing boneless animals, for instance brine shrimps (*Artemia*) or mealworms (*Tenebrio sp*), can develop observation and interpretation skills as well as learning about structure and behaviour, and indeed, scientific method (Tomkins and Tunnicliffe, 2001, 2007; Tunnicliffe, 2011, 2016). Artemia is a crustacean but has existed since the Triassic period of geological time, and is thus a living fossil! Dinosaurs may have lived in the same places as the brine shrimp. These invertebrates may be kept in an ecosystem in a one litre plastic drinking bottle with a screw top. Mealworms (*Tenebrio sp*), the small ones, are low maintenance. They are easy to keep at home or in a classroom. You can buy them at pet shops in the UK. They are used by fisherman as bait. They are excellent animals to keep in a classroom and children can make interesting observations. They are low cost, low maintenance and have no known health hazards (for further information and advice refer to www.cleapss.org.uk).

Children, particularly girls, may express disgust at first sight, but my experience is that they soon become intrigued and involved. One girl whom I taught expressed disgust but allowed me to place a mealworm larva on her open hand; she suddenly stopped grimacing and exclaimed that she could feel the power of the animal as it moved across her hand. She was full of 'awe and wonder' and then became more engaged (Tunnicliffe, 2016). The more children observe animals, the more they notice and begin learning (Tomkins and Tunnicliffe, 2007).

Keeping children's observations and interpretations

Recording children's impressions and observations is important for all concerned. A popular method, other than audio recording of dialogue, is by drawing – these may be from the observation of live animals or the viewing of preserved specimens.

Drawings have been intimately linked with humans and communication for centuries (Katz, 2017). As a biologist I have always been intrigued about how early learners, emergent biologists, learn about organisms, for it forms the basis of the understanding of which we teachers ought to understand, so that we can scaffold their further learning based on what they *actually* know or the misinformation they have acquired. A means of eliciting that which children do understand can be through analysing their drawings. Ainsworth, Partain and Tytler (2011) assert that students will deepen their understanding if they generate their own representations. Such drawings are not observational, a direct visual-to-visual approach, but conceptual (Rybska and Boeve-De Pauw, 2018). A drawing does not reveal everything but gives an indication of what the individual, in this case a young learner, understands in as much as they can draw the information. Sometimes a child will say that they cannot draw what they want to. However, analysing learner's drawings can be useful for educators in providing some of what children think of both the external and internal structure of animals, other than humans. Discussions between the teacher and the child may elicit further information and clarify what they were trying to represent. This is not always possible and is dependent on a shared language, whereas a symbol in a drawing is a universal key.

Observation in early years children is essential for the development of emergent scientists – it is one of the most important skills to be acquired (Johnston, 2005). Children's interest in local organisms can be enhanced through the observation of nature (Lindemann-Matthies, 2005). They may learn where particular animals live and how those animals adapt to various habitats (Patrick et al, 2013). Children know, for example, from their very earliest years that fish live in water. This knowledge may be acquired from stories and accompanying illustrations in books, for example, *Fish is Fish* (Lionni, 1970), or by viewing fish in an aquarium, pond or other body of water. They also notice flying organisms in everyday life, usually birds or flying insects.

The observation of living things and attitudes towards animals may also be influenced by cultural factors and emotional reactions such as fear and distaste. Prokop and Tunnicliffe (2008) documented fear and distaste towards bats and spiders amongst Slovakian children. Kellert and Westervelt (1984) determine that some conception of the environment must be in place before learners formed attitudes towards that environment and its animals. Prokop (2018) notes that the rapid response of people to animals that pose a threat of predation or sickness has evolved in humans and ensured their survival. Prokop found that children responded rapidly to predators and disease carrying organisms, particularly those displaying warning colouration such as black and yellow stripes and bright reds and oranges.

External parts of animals – the outside body patterns of vertebrates (animals with bones)

Invertebrates have relatively unfamiliar body forms, unlike the more familiar patterns of vertebrates which are more easily identifiable with a child's own body, and children, as well as certain vertebrates (for example snakes and bats), often express distaste of certain invertebrates (Looy and Wood, 2006; Prokop and Tunnicliffe, 2008). We believe this may be because their external morphology and behaviours are not as familiar as that of the vertebrates that children are familiar with, however, invertebrates do attract children's curiosity, as many primary teachers and parents will testify. Young children delight in turning over stones to see what lives beneath, most frequently small earthworms, slugs, centipedes and woodlice. These experiences may, some researchers feel, contribute to further scientific achievement.

There is relatively little published about children's understanding of vertebrates, for example Tunnicliffe and Reiss (1999), and even less on invertebrates. However, Prokop, Prokop and Tunnicliffe (2008), Rbyska et al. (2014) and Tunnicliffe (2016), have all researched and written on the understanding held by children of the internal anatomy of invertebrates.

The vertebrate pattern is more easily recognisable and identified as it has a distinct familiar pattern. Namely, a longitudinal, rounded, rectangle body, four limbs, one at each corner, a head at the front end which leads as the animal moves, and a tail at the other end, over an exit of the tube representing the gut or digestive system.

Learning from pets

Prokop, Prokop and Tunnicliffe (2008) found, through analysing data which included 1,541 drawings made by children in Slovakia, that looking after pets had advantages. Keepers of pets learned factual and conceptual knowledge of their pet and the minds of animals, as well as developing the animal's social interactions. Additionally, these young animal keepers acquired a biological understanding. The study found that pet-keeping children knew more about the internal organs of their pet than did the non-pet-keepers. However, their understanding of invertebrates was sparse. Inagaki (1990) studied Japanese children who kept goldfish. Keeping goldfish taught the children more about care and internal anatomy than that learnt by non-goldfish keeping children. Moreover, children who kept fish could predict from their knowledge the internal anatomy of other vertebrate animals, for example a frog.

Children very readily crawl along the floor, like a four-legged animal, but understand that to see where they are going, they cannot keep their neck straight but must bend it inwards. Ask children how many animals have a short straight neck, examine photographs and videos or observe live animals and notice where their head is in relation to their torso; most have a neck of some form with their head at the end arranged at such an angle that they can see in front of themselves. Observe, for example, a giraffe and a tortoise. It is an interesting activity to ask children to pretend to be a four-legged animal and then ask them why they have difficulty seeing if they keep their neck straight, in its usual position when they are upright. What do other two-legged animals do?

Sometimes they mimic being certain boneless animals, such as worms or caterpillars and wriggle along the floor. I have on occasion witnessed youngsters pretending to be butterflies, with the aid of a floaty piece of material across their shoulders and grasped in their hands while they flap the edges up and down to simulate a butterfly. Such replication play indicates that these children do indeed notice salient features and behaviours of animals they see.

Only mammals have external ear flaps. Seals are the exception, they do not have ears. If you look at a bird's head for example, you can see the opening for the inner ear like a stretched membrane, called the ear drum (which moves when it receives sound waves) as a round, covered hole at either side of their head. This may also be seen on amphibians.

One way you can find out what children observe about how animals look is from their drawings. When children draw an animal it is either from their memory, imagination or by looking at an animal directly. The external features that the children notice are what they usually show in such drawings and are the features which help them recognise the type of animal. We know from other work (e.g. Tunnicliffe, 1996) and from comments made out loud when children look at animals in exhibits, zoos or at natural history museums or even on farms, that they notice obvious features. The younger the child the simpler the observation. This recognition of the very basic shapes but gradually seeing more and more detail of external features increases with the age and understanding of a child. Drawings show the same progression.

Torkar et al. (2018) studied primary children's understanding of the external morphology of owls in Slovenia. The drawings of owls by primary aged children in Slovenia showed the external features the children knew and drew. I have invariably found that young children will draw a composition of an animal in its habitat when asked to draw external features used in deciding what is the animal's name. As they grow, older children's drawings of a named animal continue to have more and more features of the animal and become more realistic (see Figure 2.1, p. 15). Both vertebrates and invertebrates drawn by young children appear to reflect only the various obvious features. Butterflies, for example, have two body parts and only two wings – each made of two lobes. Land-living boned animals that are typically drawn are of mammals, and are shown as having a rectangular body, four legs at the corners, a tail and a head, usually with ears. The drawings appear to be influenced, at least to some extent in Western children, by images seen on the various forms of media, often with anthropomorphic features. The same applies to any models children may construct, for example from play dough.

Outside body pattern of boneless (invertebrate) animals

The invertebrates are the group of animals without bones but with different forms of skeleton. Their body pattern is not so clearly defined and depends on different groups. The number of parts of the body and legs are a key feature to watch for. Arthropods, for example, all have hard outside skeletons, think of crabs or beetles. Insects, for instance, which belong to the Arthropod groups, have three parts to their body, head, a middle part called the thorax (we call our thorax our chest) and abdomen. Insect legs are attached to their thorax and there are three on each side. One of the misunderstandings possessed by adults and children is that insects, usually typified by an adult butterfly (imago), have wings and legs attached to the abdomen. Spiders (Arachnids) have two parts to their body, a head and thorax as one, called the cephalothorax, then a more rounded abdomen. Spiders have four pairs of legs attached to their cephalothorax.

Crustaceans, another group of Arthropods, e.g. lobsters and crabs, have jointed legs. All crustaceans have five pairs of legs. This group contains small pond or sea water animals as well as larger animals. The tiny water-living animals, such as water fleas (*Daphnia* sp.), which are often used as food for fish, provide an example. Crabs, shrimps and lobsters live in water, but woodlice, common under stones and in damp places in colder climates where there is moisture, live on land. (However, there is also a freshwater woodlouse, *Asellus aquaticus*). Millipedes and centipedes are also arthropods but belong to a different group of insects.

Another invertebrate animal group is the segmented worms. Animals in this group most often seen are earthworms in temperate climates. They have a fluid skeleton on which their muscles push.

Mollusc is one of the largest groups of boneless animals and they mainly live in water, although children are probably more familiar with the land-livers, slugs and snails. One group or class is the Gastropods, slugs and snails, many of which are land livers.

 Talk science: boneless animals

Have the children noticed any boneless animals, and if so which ones? What time of the year is it? Do older children remember seeing more boneless animals such as butterflies or bees, daddy long-legs, spiders, beetles e.g. ladybirds, at certain times of the year? Why?

 Activity: 'i-spy' boneless animals

Find a notebook and a digital camera if possible.
Record what, when and where you see a boneless animal.
Take photographs if possible, print them and fix them in your Nature Notebook.

32 Learning about other animals

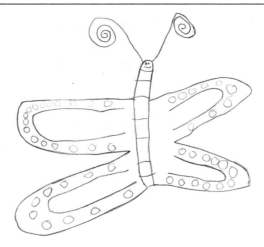

Figure 3.1 A butterfly drawn by a 5-year-old girl from Brazil

> Write the information down as field scientists do, of when, where and what, and any other comments such as the weather, next to the picture. Do you see the same animal in the same place or not? Why is that? The above can be repeated for all animals.

An activity often carried out with young children is making 'butterfly' prints from painting an outline on one half of a piece of paper, folding it in half to obtain a mirror image. This is also an activity used in maths work when we are exploring symmetry and images. The expectation is that only very basic shapes are used. It is useful to point this out to children by looking at pictures of real butterflies.

A study of 4- to 6-year-old children in a region of Brazil highlighted that their understanding of what an insect is was mainly contextual and some children took spiders and scorpions to be insects (Bartoszeck and Tunnicliffe, 2017a). Natural science in pre-school years in Brazil is poorly covered. Practical classes with insects are seldom performed and field trips are rare. This is not an uncommon situation in other countries besides Brazil. This study found that young children think these adult insects had two parts of their body and wings and legs were attached to the second part of the body, which resembled, in fact, the third part which is the abdomen. Children end up merging the two parts. They often also merge the wings into one form with two lobes instead of two separate wings.

Activity: draw an insect

Find out what your children think. All you need is a piece of paper, usually A4 size, and a pencil. Ask the child words to the effect: 'Please draw on the sheet of paper an insect which you have seen and/or what "insect" means to you'. If the understanding of internal organs is the subject, change the wording. If working with a group of children ask them not to peek at another child's drawing.

Recognising boneless animals

Children recognise boneless animals as they do boned animals by their shape, parts that stick out, and by colour and activity. Insects and worms are the most frequently referred to invertebrates (boneless animals) in my experience. Hence, insects are often called 'bugs', which is scientifically incorrect, as is the term 'minibeasts'. A school inspector, who was also a biologist, coined the term, because she said that primary teachers and children could not manage the term 'invertebrates' (Collis, 1989, personal communication). I remarked that I disagreed, because in my experience, both teachers and children are quite capable of using and understanding it, but the term 'boned' and 'non-boned' might be a useful half-way term.

True 'bugs' are separate insect groups. Children can recognise and name animals from their distinctive shapes, colours and behaviour: butterflies, bees, wasps and ladybirds. Thus, true bugs belong to the order Hemiptera. They have a piercing mouth like those of a greenfly, which belongs to a family called Aphidian (the aphids) and suck juice out of plants. They are not from the same group of insects as mosquitos or fleas, which suck blood.

The following list of the external characteristics of an insect is a useful guide for assessing children's understanding of insect's external features that can be seen while observing the insect. It is an interesting exercise to find which characteristic children find most obvious and, therefore, important when they call something an insect. Size and where they have seen the insect is also important.

- Three pairs of legs used for moving – walking or jumping.
- Three parts to the body: head, thorax and abdomen.
- Exoskeleton, hard outside.
- Anus at the end and no tail.
- Compound eyes.
- Two pairs of wings (attached to second body part).
- A pair of antennae on the head.
- Complete (incomplete) metamorphosis (egg/larvae/(nymph)/pupae/imago).
- Needs food, air and moisture to live.

Data from a study conducted in Brazil (Bartoszeck and Tunnicliffe, 2017a) shows that these South American children held a concept comparable with similarly aged North American pupils, indicating a universal development of the concept 'insect' (Barrow, 2002; Shepardson, 2002). In the Brazilian study, the most frequently mentioned insects were butterfly, beetle, ant and bee. Drawings showed a general insect pattern, sometimes with many legs, antennae and wings.

Young children often draw features of a human face on images they construct of other kinds of animals. The image created by a young boy in Brazil of an insect (Figure 3.2) unusually shows three parts to the body and three pairs of legs, but only one pair of wings. (Some flies, called the *diptera*, do only have one pair of functional wings, the second pair are so reduced and they form balance-like structures next to the first pair of wings.)

Animals which belong to the *Coleoptera*, the beetle group that includes ladybirds, have one pair of functional wings. The first pair has become hardened and forms the hard covering, the wing case, over the second operational pair that actually propel the

Figure 3.2 The outside of an insect drawn by a 5-year-old boy from Brazil

animal through the air. When they land the second pair of wings folds up and the wing cases close over them. This is easily observed when a ladybird flies and lands, as it is with any other beetle. A 5-year-old Brazilian boy drew the insect in Figure 3.2 more accurately than is more usually seen, as part of this study. The arrow on the drawing seems to indicate a location unknown to us! Interviewing can also elucidate such points of enquiry.

Inside animals with bones and without – hole though the middle internal anatomy

Hole through the middle

We humans, like all animals above the 'worm' level, are triploblastic – three layered animals with a gut from an 'entry' (mouth) to an 'exit' hole. The evolution of a 'through' gut was a breakthrough in animal evolution as animals became three-layered, in contrast to their two-layered ancestors such as the jellyfish group. Essentially, the basic body plan is a tube with two layers built around it – the body cavity containing organs with an external cover, the skin. On entry, food could be processed as it travelled the gut, which became convoluted and differentiated; waste was stored at the end of this long tube in what we call the rectum and voided through the hole (anus) which, in mammals, is controlled by muscles (the sphincter). Unlike two-layered animals, where food enters into the body through one hole and waste is ejected from the same opening, for example as in jellyfish and sea anemones, in three-layered animals, liquid leaves the gut via the bloodstream and the kidneys where it moves into the bladder and is eventually excreted. Not all animals have two body openings (one for food to go in and one for wastes to leave). Jellyfish and sea anemones for example have one multipurpose opening to their body. Animals from the worm level upwards all have two openings, as do we humans.

Talk science: hole through the middle

Ask, where does our food go? How does it enter our body and move through us? Why don't we burst when we are always putting in more and more food? Where does our drink go? Why don't we swell up with it all?

 Activity: tube through your middle model!

You may need: Tubes, paper, tissue, pencil, glue and paper straws.

Ask the children how they think they could make a simple model to show the basic pattern of a three-layered animal like them, with an outside and an inside arranged around a tube through its middle, with an 'in' for food and an 'out' for waste. Collect the items needed once they have worked out their idea.

One idea is to construct or use a cardboard tube, such as toilet tissue, tissue paper or other 'filler' and a smaller diameter tube, either a paper straw of a tube made from rolling a piece of paper around a pencil and fixing the loose side with glue or tape. Insert the paper tube (representing the gut) inside the card tube (the outer body covering) and fill the space between it with the filler. Some children like to add arms and legs and a head made of paper and colour it. If you can bend the 'gut' tube it can exit through the mouth in the paper face.

Earlier works of Reiss and Tunnicliffe (2001), summarised the development of an understanding of human organs (see Chapter 2). They identified a sequence while acknowledging that there were exceptions. The order of growth in knowledge about any organ, as given below, shows the typical progression of developing understanding of both anatomy and the physiology of an organ. They also stated the limitations of looking at drawings alone, because drawings and the interviews complement each other. For knowledge that cannot be or is difficult to verbalise, drawings can be especially useful in assessing the understanding of the child. The information may be supplemented by an interview. This is particularly helpful with younger children, especially if there are no labels, which it would be unusual to have on drawings by young children. Overall, drawings provide a focus for interviews and children will offer much more using the drawing as a cue to dialogue. Even university undergraduates said that they found trying to draw a system on which you indicate its functions was challenging.

The development sequence suggested of how children learn about internal anatomy is:

1. Awareness of organ.
2. Knowledge of name of organ.

3. Knowledge of (approximate) correct position of organ.
4. Knowledge of one function of organ.
5. Appreciation that organ has more than one function.
6. Understanding that organ relates to other organs.

(Tunnicliffe and Reiss, 2006)

Inside animals without bones

There has been little work on children's ideas of the inside organs of boneless animals. A few published studies are summarised here. We know that children use themselves as the pattern as they start interpreting their everyday world, including themselves. Hence, it is not surprising that they initially assume that all other animals have the same functions and parts. Young children use themselves as the template for other animals. Vertebrate organs are often indicated inside invertebrates. In a study by Tunnicliffe and Reiss (2001a, 2001b), who asked children from year 5 up to Cambridge undergraduates to draw the internal organs of a crab, nearly all drawings, even those by biology and education undergraduates, drew bones, although the exoskeleton of a crab, its hard, outer covering was clearly obvious! Most drawings also included lungs, indicating an awareness of the drawer that some respiratory mechanisms should be inside the crab and, as they were unaware what was the appropriate structure, drew what they knew to be a respiratory organ.

A class of 7-year-old pupils in a primary school in an English town had, in the previous year in their primary school, kept a wormery and observed the earthworm inhabitants in action. They were asked, with the usual instructions, to draw what they thought was inside an earthworm, as shown in Figure 3.3.

The children had kept a wormery in the previous school year. Their class teacher cued them in by talking about the wormery and what the worms did. There were 28 children in the class. Out of these children, only two boys and five girls, one of whom also

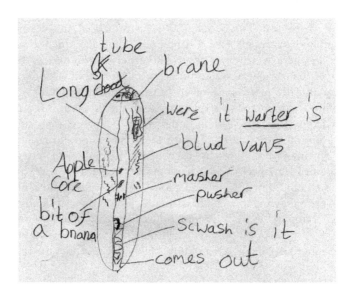

Figure 3.3 Drawing by an 8-year-old boy showing the inside of an earthworm

mentioned a mouth, correctly drew the gut. Others misplaced the gut, having it beginning behind the central ganglion (counted as brain if that is as it was labelled), but with no obvious opening. A few drew lungs, which showed that some of this class had an understanding that worms needed to breathe and a few drawings showed an awareness of the need for an excretory organ. However, only one child (female), drew an external view showing segmentation.

Blood in the body cavity was indicated in several drawings, as was a heart, and one girl also drew a gut with an opening and an anus, while another child labelled different parts of the gut as 'masher, pusher, squashes it out'.

A class of the same age in another local school had never kept a wormery and had little knowledge of earthworms. They did not realise that the animals had a through gut, which the other class nearly all did because they said they had watched the worms eating, pulling leaves into their burrows and the development of worm castes.

A similar mixed understanding is revealed in drawings of other invertebrates – a crab and a snail

The drawings of children showing their understanding of the internal organs of boneless animals discussed so far shows us that children use the 'template' of themselves to interpret other animals (Bartozeck and Tunnicliffe, 2017b). An interesting finding from snail drawings of 7-year-old Polish children (Rybska et al., 2014) was that they drew organs in the foot of the snail and three literally drew a 'home', as they understood the term (a bedroom with curtains at the window) inside the shell. Such an understanding is possibly gained from early children's literature, which refers to the snail carrying its home on its back. 'Home' is taken literally by the children as a home like theirs. They do not learn that animals have homes suitable for them, serving the same function as our human homes. It is, as it is in other animals, a place to live, such as a burrow, and is a place of refuge. A snail's shell is a protection, from attackers and from the dry atmosphere.

Inside animals with bones

Tunnicliffe and Reiss (2001) looked at the drawings of the inside of a fish, a bird and a rat, as well as a human, and found the use of the human template.

Drawings of fish often had a classic fish-shaped outline, as highlighted in Figure 3.4. This drawing shows that the young child knew the animal needed a brain, a stomach and bones. Sometimes, but rarely, a child drew the iconic fish skeleton that is often depicted in cartoons.

Birds were also drawn following the human template (see Figure 3.5). As in drawings of other boned animals, bird drawings by the youngest children (5 years of age) were often portrayed with dog-bone-shaped images – very characteristic of early learners – arranged around the inside of the periphery of the drawn body cavity.

Children seem to find mammals the easiest animals to draw and in which to insert organs. Figure 3.6 is unusual in that it indicates that the child had an understanding of mammalian pregnancy, unless it also indicates that large animals eat smaller ones of their own kind, again illustrating the benefits of interviewing a child after each one has finished their drawing. This drawing also shows how this child orientated their knowledge of their internal organs to the axis of the animal they were drawing. It shows an anthropomorphic face, very often drawn by younger children, along

38 Learning about other animals

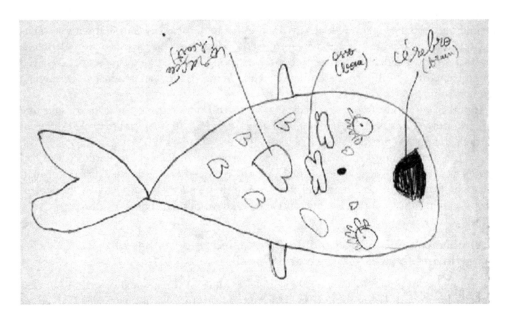

Figure 3.4 Drawing of a fish by a pre-school-aged boy from Brazil

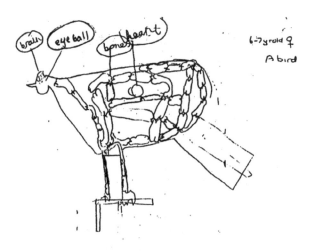

Figure 3.5 An 11-year-old pupil's drawing of the internal organs of a bird

with the other iconic shapes, such as a heart and a 'dog bone' shape drawn by the youngest learners once they have progressed beyond the 'straight line' stage. I considered that it was probably representative of the child's understanding that dogs like to eat bones, as this type of drawing is often seen in early learners.

The young boy who drew the dog in Figure 3.6 also drew another dog (a Scottie) sitting up, resting on its hind quarters. In that drawing the child could insert the organs, just like in the position of a human.

Figure 3.6 Drawing of a dog

 Talk science: inside pets

What animals do you know? Do you have a pet or do you know someone's pet? What kind is it? What do you think this pet has inside them? Why should it need anything inside? Why do you have organs? How do you think these inside parts are arranged and what do you think they are? What is their job?

Conclusion

Young children become aware of animals in their immediate environment, like pets or domesticated animals. They also notice animals of the natural world, such as earthworms, birds and insects. They become aware of differences in form and behaviour as well as the needs and habitats of the variety of animals they see. Initially animals that move attract the child's attention and, as they learn, they may indicate the presence of a plant to explain the animal's habitat or food supply. Chapter 4 focuses on children and plants.

References

Ainsworth, S., Partain, V. and Tytler, R. (2011) Drawing to learn science. *Science*, 333(6046): 1096–1097, 26 August.
Allen, M. (2015) Preschool children's taxonomic knowledge of everyday species. *Journal of Research in Science Teaching*, 52(1): 107–134.

Barrow, L.H. (2002) What do elementary students know about insects? *Journal of Elementary Science Education*, 14(2): 53–60.

Bartoszeck, A.B. and Tunnicliffe, S.D. (2017a) Development of biological literacy through drawing organisms. In Katz, P. (ed), *Drawing for Science Education: An International Perspective*. Rotterdam: Sense Publications, pp. 55–65.

Bartoszeck, A.B. and Tunnicliffe, S.D. (2017b) What do children think is inside a crab? *Journal of Emergent Science*, 13: 20–28, Summer.

Collis, M. (1989) Personal communication.

Felgenhauer, B.E. (1992) Internal anatomy of the decapoda: an overview. In Harrison, R. and Humes, A. (eds), *Microscopic Anatomy of Invertebrates*. Hoboken: Wiley-Liss, pp. 45–75.

Freeman, W.H. and Bracegirdle, B. (1971) *An Atlas of Invertebrate Structure*. London: Heinemann Educational.

Ghazali, Z. and Tolmie, A. (2014) New approaches to understanding the development of biological concepts in young children. *Education Siglo XXI*, 32(2): 97–118.

Inagaki, K. (1990) The effects of raising animals on children's biological knowledge. *British Journal of Developmental Psychology*, 8(1): 119–129.

Johnston, J. (2005) *Early Explorations in Science*. Maidenhead, UK: Open University Press, p. 33.

Katz, P. (2017) Preface. In Katz, P. (ed), *Drawing for Science Education: An International Perspective*. Rotterdam: Sense, pp. vii.

Kellert, S.R. and Westervelt, M.O. (1984) Children's attitudes, knowledge and behaviors towards animals. *Children's Environments Quarterly*, 1(3): 8–11.

Korfiatis, K. and Tunnicliffe, S. (2012) The living world in the curriculum: ecology, an essential part of biology learning. *Journal of Biological Education*, 46(3): 125–127.

Lindemann-Matthies, P. (2005) 'Loveable' mammals and 'lifeless' plants: how children's interest in common local organisms can be enhanced through observation of nature. *International Journal of Science Education*, 27(6): 655–677.

Lionni, L. (1970) *Fish Is Fish*. New York: Pantheon Press.

Looy, H. and Wood, J.R. (2006) Attitudes towards invertebrates: are educational 'bug' banquets effective? *The Journal of Environmental Education*, 37(2): 37–48.

Patrick, P., Byrne, J., Tunnicliffe, S.D., Asunta, T., Carvalho, G.S., Havu-Nuutinen, S., Sigurjónsdóttir, H., Óskarsdóttir, G. and Tracana, R.B. (2013) Students (ages 6, 10 and 15 years) in six countries knowledge of animals. *NorDiNa*, 9(1): 1–15.

Prokop, P. (2018) Natural selection influences the reactions of children to potentially dangerous animals. *Eurasia Journal of Mathematics, Science & Technology Education*, 14(4): 1398–1406.

Prokop, P., Prokop, M. and Tunnicliffe, S.D. (2008) Effects of keeping animals as pets on children's concepts of vertebrates and invertebrates. *International Journal of Science Education*, 30(4): 431–449. DOI: 10.1080/09500690701206686.

Prokop, P. and Tunnicliffe, S.D. (2008) 'Disgusting' animals: primary school children's attitudes and myths of bats and spiders. *Eurasia Journal of Mathematics, Science & Technology Education*, 4(2): 87–97.

Reiss, M.J. and Tunnicliffe, S.D. (2001) Students' understandings of human organs and organ systems. *Research in Science Education*, 31(3): 383–399.

Rybska, E. and Boeve-De Pauw, J. (2018) Drawings on biology. How can drawings help to conceptualise flowers? Presentation given at European Researchers in Didactics of Biology Conference, 4 July, Zaragoza, Spain.

Rybska, E., Tunnicliffe, S.D. and Sajkowska, Z.A. (2014) Young children's ideas about snail internal anatomy. *Journal of Baltic Science Education*, 13(6): 828–838.

Shepardson, D.P. (2002) Bugs, butterflies, and spiders: children's understandings about insects. *International Journal of Science Education*, 24(6): 627–643.

Spektor-Levy, O., Barrpsuch, Y.K. and Mevarech, Z. (2011) Science and scientific curiosity in pre-school – the teacher's point of view. *International Journal of Science Education*, 35(13): 1–28.

Tomkins, S.P. and Tunnicliffe, S.D. (2001) Looking for ideas: observation, interpretation and hypothesis-making by 12-year-old pupils undertaking science investigations. *International Journal of Science Education*, 23(8): 791–813.

Tomkins, S. and Tunnicliffe, S.D. (2007) Nature tables: discovering children's interest in natural objects. *Journal of Biological Education*, 41: 150–151.

Torkar, G., Gnidovec, T., Tunnicliffe, S.D. and Tomažič, I. (2018) Assessing students' knowledge about owls from their drawings and written responses. *Journal of Biological Education*, 28(1): 269–277.

Tunnicliffe, S.D. (1996) A comparison of conversations of primary school groups at animated, preserved and live animal specimens. *Journal of Biological Education*, 30(3): 1–12.

Tunnicliffe, S.D. (2011) Young children as emergent biologists: brine shrimps in the classroom. *Journal of Emergent Science*, 1(2): 25–32.

Tunnicliffe, S.D. (2016) Observing mealworms in the primary classroom. *Journal of Emergent Science*, 11: Summer: 23–37.

Tunnicliffe, S.D., Gatt, S., Agius, A. and Pizzuto, S.A. (2008) Animals in the lives of young Maltese children. *Eurasia Journal of Mathematics, Science & Technology Education*, 4(3): 215–221.

Tunnicliffe, S.D. and Reiss, M.J. (1999) Building a model of the environment: how do children see animals? *Journal of Biological Education*, 33(4): 142–148.

Tunnicliffe, S.D. and Reiss, M.J. (2001) What's inside bodies? learning about skeletons and other organ systems of vertebrate animals. In Valanides, N. (ed), *Proceedings of the 1st Symposium of the International Organisation for Science and Technology Education in Southern Europe*. Paralimni, Cyprus: Imprinta, pp. 84–94.

Tunnicliffe, S.D. and Reiss, M.J. (2006) Drawing breath: the use of drawings and interviews in a six-year longitudinal study of 5–11-year-olds' understandings of what is inside themselves. Paper given at ERIDOB (European Researchers in Didactics of Biology) Conference, London.

Tunnicliffe, S.D. and Ueckert, C. (2011) Early biology: the critical years for learning. *Journal of Biological Education*, 45(4): 173–175.

Chapter 4

Learning about plants

Introduction

Biological awareness and interpretation are unlike other aspects in the world of a child in which they are constructing knowledge and interpreting the world in their terms. A child, and any human being, is a part of the biological world rather than an observer of it, as humans are of the physical world (Hadzigeorgiou, 2015). Young children explain phenomena through applying 'personalisation', explaining biological phenomena in personal terms, especially the more similar the target for interpretation is to the child themselves. Plants are a much neglected area in the curriculum, and that is why children have a poor understanding of the internal organisation of plants (Bartoszeck, Cosmo, da Silva and Tunnicliffe, 2015). Plants are an important part of the scenery of children's lives, however, some young children (aged 5) did not consider trees to be living organisms (Rybska, Sajkowska and Tunnicliffe, 2014).

Children explain structures and behaviours in plants by recognising similarities to themselves to interpret what they observe or are asked. Sanders and Jenkins (2018) consider that the optimum way of learning about plants is to look at real ones.

 Talk science: plants and you

Which plants are taller than you that you know of? Which are shorter than you? Which are wider? Which lie across the ground? Which grow upright?

 Activity: how tall?

Ask each child to measure the height of an herbaceous plant.

Ask them what they could use to measure it and provide, if possible, what they request. Useful items could be lengths of wool, ribbon or string, a metre rule or ruler, strips of squared paper and crayons, so they can mark the height of the plant on the paper and colour in the squares. They could produce a wall bar chart, either as an individual or as part of a group.

> The differing measurements can be lain on a flat surface and arranged in order of height (providing you know which height measure refers to which plant, so adult assistance is vital in recording this). A discussion about the order of the measurements can develop if you wish. Ask, 'what do these results mean?' 'Is there a pattern as to where the tallest or shortest plants grow and why is this?'

Plants, including trees, are all around – on paths, in vegetable and fruit shops, as decorations in homes, as foods and as images on clothes, soft furnishings, wallpapers and fabrics. Children can see images of plants in a number of different forms, such as birthday cards, wrapping paper, fabrics, soft toys and emblems, like the stylised image of a rose flower being used for the English Rugby team logo on the team shirts or leeks and daffodils being emblems of the country of Wales.

Plant anatomy

> **Talk science: parts of plants**
>
> What have you noticed about plants? What are the biggest plants you have seen? The smallest? How do plants stay upright? What do you think they have inside them? What items could children use to estimate the heights of plants? Do older children have different ideas to younger children? How are their ideas different? If you have the materials, let children test their hypotheses.

> **Activity: plant walk**
>
> Take a plant walk in the garden, a park or along a path. Suggest that the children find, say, five plants bigger than themselves and five plants smaller; are any the same size as them? How can they measure this? What methods can the children work out?

Asking a group of 7 year olds what was inside a tree standing by the perimeter fence of our school, they drew what they thought on a drawing. Muscles, according to two of the seven children, held up branches of trees and all children considered that trees had a heart inside the middle of their trunk (Tunnicliffe, 1999).

What do your children think? These children were using their knowledge of themselves to explain the inside of the tree. If you ask children this question ensure you define what you mean by 'inside', as I have found that often early years children, and even older children, really mean the area inside the canopy of the tree, which is covered by leaves when you look from the outside, rather than actually inside the branches themselves (just as our bones, for example, are beneath the skin and not just inside our clothes).

Born inquirers

Children are born inquirers and problem solvers, usually inherently interested in the world and other living organisms with whom they share it. In other words, they are emergent biologists. Much of what children know about plants is learnt by themselves and from family, friends and media, such as books and television. They understand that they are static, and that they grow and disappear, unlike other animals. Later, emergent biologists (5–10 years of age) possess inquiring minds and apply this to the study of living organisms (Schreck Reiss et al., 2014). Children are so interested and surrounded by biology in action that it might be considered the most accessible science for early learners (Patrick and Tunnicliffe, 2011). My late father, a biologist, held that botany was the 'Queen' of the sciences, and ever present. He asserted that it was the most accessible discipline of the biological sciences for the naturalist, which is the role that young children assume.

Little work has been done on the early experiences of children looking at plants. Sanders and Jenkins (2018) point out that adaptations of plants (and plants in general) are most effectively learned when looking at real plants. In a study of children aged 5–14, it was shown that they could recognise and name plants, they knew anatomical features of plants and they understood specialised habitats (Tunnicliffe and Reiss, 2000). Compared to animals, however, their knowledge of plants is more restricted (Gatt et al., 2007); children's books feature animals far more than plants. A botanic garden in Portugal produced a book focused on the story of their garden, which has been translated into many languages (Tavares, 2013), but that is unusual. Some fiction books may illustrate the life cycle of a seed, for instance, the well-known story, *Jack and the Beanstalk*.

Children have some everyday knowledge of everyday plants (Patrick and Tunnicliffe, 2011). They begin learning about plants and plant parts in the home, particularly in relation to food. My eldest son, Alan, knew five plant-related words in his first 50 words. I wrote each new piece of vocabulary down when I heard him say it for the first time. The words were utilitarian – orange, pineapple, lawn, beans and onion (Tunnicliffe, 2013).

Children can identify plants they see on their way to and from school (Lindemann-Mathies, 2006), in their homes and gardens, in the countryside and in the media. Sanders (2007) stated that gardening is the most often cited recreational pastime of the British and, indeed, children will tell you about gardening with their family if they take part. In a study of children's understanding of everyday plants, children were aware of houseplants, but in work I carried out they could not name them other than descriptively (Tunnicliffe and Reiss, 2001). A 7-year-old girl explained after being shown a house plant (a miniature rose), 'It's a house plant, it's in a plant pot'; an 11-year-old said, 'A houseplant, like the plant that grows at home in a basket, it's got little flowers'.

In an exploratory study conducted in Brazil, children aged between 3 and 10 years old (kindergarten and primary school), the majority of them between 4 and 5 years old (total 145), were asked to draw what they thought was a plant (total sample = 332). An equal number of boys and girls were asked by their teacher to join in the task so that all abilities were included, and asked to list which plants they knew and where they had seen them. The answers showed that the children knew about local plants and were in touch with nature. I have also found the same responses in England several times (Unpublished data, which contributed to Tunnicliffe and Reiss, 2000).

Talk science: plants we see

Talk about which plants or parts of plants you see together every day. Describe the plants you see growing as you walk to school or visit other places.

When does your plant have leaves? Spring, summer, autumn, winter? Where are the leaves? Are there any parts of the plant on the ground now? Do you see dead leaves or twigs blowing in the wind? Do the plants look the same all year round? How many seasons does your country have? How can you tell when the seasons change?

 Talk science: my plant

Choose a plant that interests the children. How do you know which ones they are interested in? Ask them. What was it that interested them? Was it their colour, which you liked, their leaves, do the leaves have a leaf stalk? Are they arranged on one stem or on side stems? What is their shape? What are the edges like? How does it smell? How does it feel when you touch it? Why is the stem rough when you feel the trunk or smooth or hairy like some herbal plants?

Keeping an observation record

At differing times of year, and as a child grows, they notice different aspects of the same plants kept or observed. It may be useful to you, and to them when older, to reflect on the previous comments after they have made a new group of plants. Thus, keeping a record can yield interesting dialogues subsequent to visits.

 Activity: plant walk journal

Make a plant walk journal. You will need a notebook, an electronic tablet or similar and coloured pencils or crayons. Construct a 'my everyday plant photo log' in your notebook or on your tablet. Photograph the plant you like best (or worst) and decide to study it all year. Justify your reasons for choosing this plant. Explain why you like or dislike it.

Photograph it when you begin. If you can, print the photograph then name the plant and note where it was seen. Perhaps photograph other plants of interest. Write the observations under the relevant photograph, along with the date. Observe the plant regularly – you decide how often you would like to observe it (daily, weekly, every four weeks etc.) – and note any differences from what you noticed before. Does the plant change each time you observe it? If so, in what ways? This activity also fits in with the next chapter about change.

How children 'see' plants

We are beginning to understand how children 'see' plants; a key part of the environment. Yet plant blindness is a recognised phenomenon, first published with a colleague after years of discussion. 'Plant blindness' was first coined by my late friend, the biologist James Wandersee, who talked about it for some years first, for the recognition of plants (Wandersee and Schussler, 1999). Plant blindness was broadly defined as 'the inability to see or notice the plants in one's own environment, leading to the inability to recognise the importance of plants in the biosphere and in human affairs'. Why does this 'plant blindness' occur in very young children? Simply, it is suggested, because the child searches for movement, conspicuous colours and patterns, objects that are known and objects that are potential threats. Since plants are static, blend in with the background, and do not eat humans, they generally do not attract attention (Allen, 2003). Louv (2006) claimed that children have lost touch with nature, a sentiment often repeated. However, while children may not understand about mega fauna and endemic wild animals of their area, they do know about local plants and animals. For example, primary school-aged children in the capital city of an African country, which has game reserves visited by tourists, were unaware of the mega fauna which European children had learned about. The children of the city did not visit the game reserves as they were the province of wealthy tourists.

Children see live animals and plants at home in gardens or backyards or on visits to zoos and botanical gardens (Sanders, 2007). Patrick and Tunnicliffe (2011) put forward two possible reasons for 'botaniphobia'. First, plants do not 'move and are also non-threatening because humans, pick out movement in animals ... which may signal danger'. Second, as we are also an animal, we have an inbuilt interest and curiosity towards other animals. I found, on taking a party of 12-year-old schoolchildren to the Princess of Wales's greenhouse in Kew Gardens, that they were fascinated by the various plants that they could see and touch, particularly the carnivorous plants, however, on seeing the movement of fish in aquaria, they rushed to view them and ignored the plants (Tunnicliffe, 2001). Plants are usually thought of as those 'things' with flowers. Trees, for example, were not recognised as plants by the children in Malta (Gatt et al., 2007), and also in other countries from my observations.

Living organisms have an important place in children's lives. Schneekloth (1989) asserted that as children develop they assume the attitude held by many adults that vegetation is utilitarian. Furthermore, while it appears that urban children in the USA were anxious about visiting natural sites, they do have some knowledge of plants from their own lives.

Plants are a key part of the environment, yet we understand little of how children perceive them, and how and why this is to a lesser extent than animals. Indeed, without plants there would be no animals as they are dependent on plants as a source of energy. No plants, no energy for animals. Energy is captured by chemicals in green plants in a process known as photosynthesis and is stored in chemicals made by the plants. They are consumed and then, in turn, are eaten by meat eating animals. Humans eat both animal material (cheese, milk and eggs contain energy, as well as meat) and plant materials. But, no plants means no animals. Historically, plants were regarded as obtaining food through their roots (Barker, 1995), an idea I have often heard repeated in primary schools. Women in rural Bangladesh were amazed to learn that plants made their own food, and the understanding of this gave these women a new respect for plants, which hitherto they had regarded as something provided for their use, not as living beings with similar needs to themselves for food. Children have an understanding of vegetation, which contributes to their understanding of their environment, and urban children have preferences for aspects of nature involving plants (Simmons, 1994). Moreover, a person's attitude towards, and understanding of 'the environment, are profoundly shaped by their attitudes towards, experiences and understandings of living organisms' (Tunnicliffe and Reiss, 1999, 2000).

 Talk science: flowers of different shapes

Ask the children if they have seen insects visiting flowers. Can they remember the kinds of insects and the flowers they were visiting? What shape were the flowers? What colour were the flowers? Can they visit a flowerbed and make observations on insects and flowers (in an appropriate season)? How can they find out more information?

Learning to recognise plants

When beginning to learn about plants, children are curious and need to acquire the vocabulary to be able to discuss plants. Providing this vocabulary is a necessary part of our role as teachers. Unlike learning parts of the human body, where children usually acquire the names in relation to themselves and their own body parts, plants are different. Children are able to recognise the main parts of a plant, for example, a stem, the leaves and flowers, but unless they see a plant out of the soil, they frequently do not realise that they have roots.

 Talk science: what happens when ... ?

Ask them why the plant has roots and note their responses. Growing a plant in soil in a see-through container will enable a child to see its extensive network of roots. You can show them this by removing a seedling from a tray of rape and cress by very carefully pulling up a plant, so that the child can examine the root system. Without this network the plant would not stay anchored in the ground and would be blown over by a strong wind. If you watch plants in a breeze, what does the child see happen? What does the child think might happen? Why do they say that? Does the plant stay in the 'posture' position it has when there is no wind? Ask what position this is usually. What happens when a breeze catches the plant or you brush against it? Does it move? Does it break off, does it fall over? Watch the branches and trunk of a tree in the wind. What happens?

Categorising trees poses a problem for many adults and children. In the English language the word 'plant' is used in everyday speech to mean 'flower', but trees are not plants, and neither are weeds! Children refer to other plants by definite group names, for example ferns and mosses and fir trees or conifers. Fungi are often referred to as 'mushrooms', whatever kind they are. Many people do not realise that fungi are not plants – plants are green whereas fungi are not, and they are unable to make their own food as green plants do. Instead they must obtain ready-made food from other living things. We increasingly know more about fungi as the refuse disposers of the living world and their vital role with trees in communication and sharing resources between trees.

Very young children are attracted to flowering plants. They like the colours and are almost 'elastically' attracted to the petals which they pull, often removing them, one by one! This 'touch and pull' instinct is similar to the desire to grab at furry animals. My eldest son carefully removed all the petals of a row of pink tulips in flower along a path. The daisy group, *Compositae*, seem to attract children the most. Leaves also attract. They are often easy to pull off the plant. Young children often make collections of such leaves and arrange them according to shape, colour and size. Alternatively, collecting sticks or pine cones also seems to fascinate children (Tunnicliffe and Ueckert, 2011).

Plants make smells. Children enjoy smelling flowers. Plant smells or odours vary from plant to plant and this is their way of communicating with others. Plants make certain odours too if they are damaged. The smell of newly cut grass is actually the smell of damage – a distress signal emitted to indicate that the plant has been damaged. Plants can also send out a distress call by making a smell that acts as a 'call' for a predatory insect to come and attack other insects that are harming the plant. Ladybirds eat greenflies, which attack plants such as beans by piercing the outer covering of the plant and sucking up the fluids with their mouth parts. Observe ladybirds eating greenfly on plants that are attacked by aphids.

Colour in plants

Educators, formal or informal, should encourage this inherent interest by developing activities which assist early learners in identifying colour, shape, size, smell and texture.

Very young children begin to identify primary colours and can develop and extend their skills by walking past flowers and naming the colours that can be seen. Set up a colour trail in an area such as a garden or flowering field and develop a 'colour hunt', perhaps with clues for older children. Provide a card with a colour on and challenge the learner to find a flower to match it. Such activities are a useful way to enforce colour understanding and encourage the child to look with purpose, to make observations, ask questions and justify their reasons for making decisions regarding colour. This activity is the beginning of working scientifically.

Numeracy and plants

The same technique can be used to identify the different variety of greens that are seen not only in leaves but also in stalks, stems and buds. Alternatively, the different shapes of the leaves on bushes, trees and herbaceous plants can be usefully matched with diagrams or basic, cut-out mathematical shapes. From a distance, an oak tree looks like a rough-edged cylinder. A Christmas tree has the basic shape of a triangle. If you stand far enough away the shape held up can obscure the plant. This 'find the shape' activity can be easily carried out with small shapes while looking at pictures in books and charts.

 Talk science: discussing results

Ask what the results from the above activity mean. Is there a pattern as to where the tallest or shortest plants grow and why is this so? Obviously, children can practice their number sequences by counting things about plants. 'How many plants of the same kind are together?' 'How many flowers are on that plant?' 'How many leaves?' These are just a few of the questions that can be posed. How many different shapes are there? Do tall insects visit all flowers? How would you answer the questions?

Shapes of flowers

There are many different shapes of flowers. Children may make up their own descriptive names for these differently shaped blossoms. Pompom-like flowers, such as flowers of the onion, are called 'dome' flowers by botanists. In the spring, children notice the trumpet shapes of daffodils and model flowers may be easily constructed with cardboard tubes.

- Rounded tops, e.g. dandelions, referred to as domed flowers.
- Flat and circular, having many petals, e.g. daisies. Petals are arranged in a circle around a central part, which is usually yellow.
- Cup-shaped, e.g. poppies and buttercups.
- Trumpet-shaped, e.g. daffodils, petals attached to a cylindrical centre.
- Irregular flowers with two matching sides if the flower were to be sliced down its middle, e.g. foxgloves, white deadnettles, pea flowers.

 Talk science: flower shapes

There are various categories of flower shape. What shapes of flowers do children notice? Round, long, flattened form, side to side? What insects have they noticed visiting the different shaped flowers? Circular or flat, cup, tubed and 'irregular', are the shapes the young most often describe.

Activity: shape search

Provide a variety of shapes and let the children match a flower to the shape. This can be done using cut-out pictures from catalogues or images downloaded from the internet, or they can be observed on real flowers at home or in school. Do children's observations tally with the shapes described by botanists?

Plants we eat

Many adults in Western societies will distinguish between plants as flowers and plants as food, whether they are vegetables or fruits. Children absorb the categorisation in everyday use. They may not find it easy to distinguish tomatoes and cucumbers as fruits (they contain seeds), so there may be some conflict between actual scientific classification and their everyday assumptions.

 Talk science: naming the parts of plants we eat

Use everyday vegetables in the classroom to help the children identify and name them correctly. Help the children to notice parts of each vegetable, such as the 'eye' of the potato, stems of celery, flowers of cauliflower and broccoli, pods of peas and broad beans, root vegetables such as swede, turnip and beetroot. Fruits can be identified, such as marrows, melons, pumpkins, squash and pine nuts. Leaves such as lettuce, cabbage and spinach.

 Talk science: vegetables as food

What vegetables do you like? When do you eat them? Have you seen any living anywhere, like perhaps a grow bag, raised bed or vegetable plot? Which vegetables do you think are the stalks or leaves of a plant? What roots of plants have you eaten?

Children's recognition of plants

Taxonomy, being able to identify different kinds of plants, is a key element of biological learning. Noticing plants is an important part of children's lives and they should be encouraged to discuss what they have seen in their own environment (Lindemann-Mathies, 2005; Patrick and Tunnicliffe, 2011). Listening to and analysing the unsolicited conversations of children is one way to find out how they notice and interpret plants. Tunnicliffe undertook visits to both botanic and horticultural gardens and recorded the children's spontaneous dialogues. These were typed and the transcripts analysed using a systemic network, which yielded the major topics of conversations. From the analysis it revealed that children talk spontaneously about the easily observed features of plants, such as colour, shape and smell, and offer past experiences about garden plants. When cued by adults or other children in the group, children talk about less obvious aspects. There were no differences between the content of conversations of groups of only boys, only girls or mixed groups. Older primary children, aged 8–12, made significantly more comments focused on plants than the younger children (Tunnicliffe, 2001). Horticultural gardens, which resembled domestic gardens more closely than botanical gardens, yielded more comments from children about gardening practices. Such comments indicate that, again, children who see these types of activity, usually at home, learn from these experiences. Another boy talked, while walking through kitchen garden plots in a well-known English horticultural garden, about the runner beans being grown and how he had helped his grandfather tie them up in their garden. Another boy admired the lawns and talked about helping to mow the lawn while an 8-year-old girl talked about helping her mother to weed the flower bed.

One of the problems for learners of plants is that there is not a single structure of a standard flowering plant, although there is a basic pattern with something fixing the plant to a surface, usually the ground, and a stem growing upwards which bears leaves and flowers.

Plant structure varies with the kind of plant, although they do have the same requirements. Trees and bushes, and weeds, which are plants where humans do not want them, are all plants. However, it usually is a flowering plant that is first learnt, partially because early years books often illustrate 'plant' with a daisy or sunflower-like plant. When children are asked to draw a flower or a plant they tend to understand and use the same two words to refer to a flower.

It is important to provide a real plant with roots and a flower to help them learn the parts as a starting point. Develop this by looking at different kinds of roots; vegetables such as carrots and swedes have one big main root called a taproot, off which come very small roots almost like thick white hairs. Turnips and beetroot for example, have swollen tap roots full of food reserves for the plant.

The structure of flowers varies according to the type, but basically flowers from plants that have two seed leaves (cotyledons) have a ring of sepals, usually green, and form the protective covering of buds over the developing petals. Petals are displayed around the centre of the flower where there are stamens (male parts of the flower which produce pollen) surrounding the female part of the flower where pollen, usually from another plant of the same kind is deposited; a process that is necessary before the fruit is formed at the base of the flower. Dandelion plants have such long taproots, which grow deep into the soil, which makes them very difficult to dig out of flowerbeds. Usually gardeners consider dandelions as a weed. If you only remove the top part of this taproot another dandelion plant soon grows from it.

The flowers of monocotyledons, one cotyledon or seed leaf in the seed, like sweet corn (which have parallel 'lines' on their leaves, unlike branched ones of the leaves of dicotyledonous plants like daisies or roses), lilies, bluebells and tulips do not have sepals. I once saw a very confused class of 7-year-olds trying to identify parts of the flowers (lilies) they had been given to examine with the drawings on the chalk board which is of a half buttercup. Buttercups are cotyledons and lilies are monocotyledons. Children may have noticed, for example, the development of a fruit from a flower on an apple tree or a bush.

In preparing to visit gardens some preliminary discussion with children is useful in focusing their attention on plants as more than 'vegetation'. Visits made with people from home or school can be rendered more useful in terms of constructing an understanding through some pre-visit activities, such as those in Table 4.1.

Braund and Reiss (2004) suggest that plant blindness is surprising in countries such as England, because it has been estimated that 20 million households have a garden. Sanders (2007) reported that the British cite gardening as their favourite pastime but, increasingly, people live in flats and high-rise buildings and are therefore without gardens.

External parts of plants

Children's spoken observations of plants are very useful in determining what they understand about them. The categories of comments made by children are summarised in Table 4.2.

Children find drawing a plant a difficult task because they really have to look closely. Frequently, when young children are asked to draw a plant from memory, they usually draw a daisy-like flower and, when asked to draw a tree, they present a 'lollipop tree' (Figure 4.1), which is similar to the way in which they abstract the basic shapes of animals at this age in their drawings.

Children will often insert a drawing of the sun when drawing plants and trees. This does not mean they understand the role of the sun in the process of energy capture and carbohydrate synthesis, but it mirrors the pictures they see in most illustrated books. Children can also draw the basic leaf shapes from their observations. Villaroel (2015) investigated the colours children chose to use when drawing plants; this varied with the age of the child.

Looking at the insides of plants

Little work has been carried out on young children's understanding of the internal anatomy of plants, although examining parts of the food we eat with them can aid their understanding. Stalks of broccoli for instance, if cut through, show the vascular bundles containing the tubes that draw water and minerals from the soil, through the roots to the leaves, stems and flowers.

 Talk science: house plants

If you pick flowers or someone gives you flowers what is the difference between cut flowers and ones growing in a pot or garden? Where do you and your family buy bunches of flowers? What do you do when you get the flowers home? Why do you think that is done? What happens if you leave cut plants without water?

Table 4.1 Initial discussion about plants

What is a plant – how do children define them?	Plants – they are not able to move so they can't chase and instead have to produce their own food from nutrients in the soil (once they have used up the food stores in their seed) and from a gas, called carbon dioxide, which they take in from the air, as well as water from the soil. Most of the plants we see are seed making plants and have roots, stems, leaves and flowers. Some are herbaceous, most of the 'flowers' we see, some are bigger and are shrubs; large plants are called trees. They all have leaves and some kind of roots. Many have flowers that turn into fruits with seeds.
Where do plants grow?	
Growing needs	What does anything need to grow? What is it like before its leaves appear? How does it find water, food and warmth? How does a growing plant get its food?
Structure	How many parts are above ground and how many below ground? How many leaves? What sort of roots? Or leaves? Where are the buds? What sort of flowers? Single, one to each stem, or many flowers, similar to the many petalled daisy? How does a plant start to grow – grow chickpeas or beans or buy a box of rape and cress and examine each seedling. Ask children to identify the parts, for example the brown seed case.
A new seedling	What does it look like? Roots, and the shoot with two green leaves, the seed leaves full of food; the parent plant which provides for the developing baby plant until it can make its own.
Making new plants (see also Chapter 5)	Some plants can make new plants by vegetative reproduction, like flowering plants that come from bulbs; some plants produce stems that grow out across the ground and where this touches the ground a new plant can grow, like strawberry plants and spider plants (a house plant).
Who needs plants?	Plants are essential for animals. They are food for everything so provide energy.
Uses of plants to humans	Provide shelter, clothing, medicine etc., food and recreation.
Are any plants adapted to life where there is little water?	Which plants do children know of which live in hot, dry places? What are they like, do they look like plants you see every day? What is similar? Is anything different?
A lot of water?	Do you know of plants that grow in soggy ground and damp places?
Are trees which keep their leaves in winter (evergreens) any different from the leaves that fall from deciduous trees?	Look at a holly leaf (evergreen) and a deciduous leaf (oak). What is the difference? What is similar?

Table 4.2 Responses to plants

1. Interpretative comments	Children say what the plant resembles.
2. Affective comments	Emotive responses such as 'Ah!' or 'Ugh'.
3. Comments about the structure	Colour, size, shape; parts that break up the outline such as horns or spikes.
4. Comments about 'behaviour'	Such as giant water lilies floating on a pond, the reaction of a plant with protective movements such as a Venus fly-trap closing when stimulated to represent a fly landing on its leaves, or mimosa leaves folding from a touch stimulus. What happens if you pick a plant and the stem becomes floppy and the flower droops? Trying to break off a young twig from a bush compared with breaking a dry, dead twig from the ground.
5. Giving the plant a name	'Plant', carnivorous plant, cactus; common names, for example, smelly plant, occasionally the botanical name.
6. Habitat and geographical region	Sometimes children will comment about the natural habitat of a plant, e.g. 'It's a desert plant' when seeing cacti, or a wet-place plant when seeing mosses.

Figure 4.1 Child's drawing of a 'lollipop' tree
From the author's research conducted in Curitiba, Brazil.

Activity: where does the water go?

You need a container filled with coloured water (use food colouring), firm sticks of young celery, two potted plants (one watered and one dry) and a large, see-through, air tight bag with string or wire closures.

Water transport bundles in a stick of celery can be shown easily by placing it in a beaker of coloured water. If you place the young stems with leaves from the middle of the celery heart and leave for several hours (preferably with a draught to increase evaporation of water from the leaves), the leaves usually turn the colour of the liquid. Indeed, some teachers/parents use a white flower, such as a carnation for this investigation. If you have made this a fair test by putting a similar sized piece of celery in clear water, ask the learners what they notice.

- Why has this happened?
- If you split the stem of the flower or celery in water what might happen, why?
- If a potted plant (such as a pelargonium – more often called a geranium) is placed inside a polythene bag without holes, water eventually collects on the inside of the bag. Where has this water come from? (Try with a dry plant as well as a well-watered plant.)
- Do the children have any explanation for where this water comes?
- Is this a fair test? Why or why not?

What children think is inside trees

Researchers have particularly looked at children's understanding of the insides of trees. Bartoszeck et al. (2015) reported that during an interview with a 4-year-old girl after she had completed her drawing, she said that inside the trunk there was timber, that roots made the tree grow, and that leaves were outside the plant on the branches. A 5-year-old boy said that the roots held the tree on the ground, preventing it from falling, that the trunk was inside the plant and that an apple is an inner part of the plant.

Rybska, Sajkowska and Tunnicliffe (2014) analysed the drawings of trees made by 5-year-old Polish children. In the manner described in Tunnicliffe and Reiss (2001) (rubric for analysing the drawings depicting the internal anatomy of an animal), they devised a scale for assessing the knowledge shown by these children of the internal arrangement of a tree (see Table 4.3). Many children will also insert external features on their drawing, so we included those in the rubric – the term 'inside' the tree is often interpreted by young children as 'within the branches' and this has to be explained explicitly to them. In my first study about trees with some 7-year-olds (Tunnicliffe, 1999), I was interested to note that some of the children thought that branches were held up by muscles and that trees, like us, had hearts. This is yet another example of children using their existing knowledge to explain phenomena.

The rubric was modified in a further Polish study (Rybska, Tunnicliffe and Sajkowska, 2016). Hollows in trees often feature in children's understanding of inside a tree and some of the Polish children were aware of the growth rings in trunks from having seen the ends of stumps and logs, again intentioned in other countries where we have worked. These opinions are recollections of the child's own experiences, as one child explained that he knew that the inside of a tree was hollow because he had seen this near his home many

Table 4.3 Level source of knowledge about trees as shown in drawings

1.	**First-hand observation remembered**
	(Resemblance to a tree)
2.	**Internal parts of a tree**
	P – tubes/pipes/roots
	H – human template – heart, lungs
	J – juices/resin/water/oxygen
	A – age/timber
	D – hollow
3.	**External parts**
	L – leaves
	F – fruit
	B – bark
	G – branches
	S – seeds
4.	**Ecological and habitat views associated**
	B – birds
	O – ants (insects)
	P – spiders
	Ps – spider web
	M – mammals (such as squirrel)
	I – other animals
5.	**Other features drawn**: e.g. indicating religion or culture influences and other biological features and explanations

Adapted from Rybska, Sajkowska and Tunnicliffe (2014)

times. Young learners are observant. They make logical assumptions – not 'misconceptions', but early learners explain to themselves and to others what they see to their own satisfaction.

The next most frequent category found was reference to many different kinds of internal fluids – from water to maple syrup. Some children literally drew water inside a tree. Polish children, living in a part of the country where irrigation is a major issue, explained that water is crucial for the tree in order to survive, and that it comes all the way from the ground to the leaves. This is not an understanding that children in other, similar studies appeared to have. In studies by Tunnicliffe (1999) and Bartoszeck et al. (2015), some pupils (13) drew human organs inside a tree, most commonly a heart. Children understood that trees keep their upward branches attached to the trunk and the explanation given for this is the possession of muscles. This is an indication of basic scientific reasoning held by the children at this stage, as is the frequency with which Polish children drew tubes inside trees to carry water to the tops. Unusually, four Polish children put 'soul' as an internal, or even external, feature of the tree.

Children whom I have worked with across the developed world seem to share basic ideas depending upon where they live and, through their activities and observations of local trees, they determine what must be inside them. The Polish children in this study (Rybska, Sajkowska and Tunnicliffe, 2014) lived in an area where irrigation was of paramount importance, hence the children knew that plants, including trees, needed water.

The same reasoning may be applied to herbaceous flowering plants. Older children have an understanding that cut flowers, garden flowers and container plants require water, otherwise their flowers will wilt and die. Children will notice drooping plants in gardens or pots when there has been little rain, particularly when the outside temperature is raised, but they do not always connect their observations with the need to supply water to replenish and revive the plants.

Fungi

Fungi have features of plants and of animals but are neither. They are grouped as a special kingdom. They are largely the great unseen organisms, which have a vital role, in particular in the decomposition of other living things and, we now know, in the life of trees in ancient woods (Wohlleben, 2017). One of the defining features of plants and animals is the structure of their cells. Plants have definite, firm cell walls, constructed mainly of cellulose, which animals do not. Fungi, like plants, do not move from place to place under their own power, as most animals do at some stage of their lives, although plants and fungi do have a mechanism that releases their seeds, or spores, into the air. Therefore, various methods of dispersal mean new organisms will grow away from the parent.

Even though fungi have defined cells, they do not have the same internal structure as that found inside the main groups of plants. Instead, they are made up of many strands called hyphae, which form tubes called mycelium. Take apart the stalk of a mushroom carefully with a needle or toothpick and these may be easily seen. Children readily notice one kind of fungi that makes its fruiting body above ground, which contains its spores, but these do not make seeds because they are not seed plants. Like the toadstools in a fairy ring, Ink cap fungi or puffballs are sometimes seen in gardens as well as in fields and woods, as is bracket fungi which can be seen on old trees, indicating that the tree is near the end of its life. We do not see the vast colonies of fungal mycelium underground forming nets of fine white strands and which, in undisturbed woodland, form a communication system between trees through which trees share food, carbon dioxide (Simard et al., 1997) and water in support of more needy trees. This network also communicates with other trees using chemical signals transited via this fungal network (Wohlleben, 2017, p. 10). Fungi grow as tubular filaments called hyphae. The mass of hyphae, a mycelium, becomes a vast organ underground and is a chemical communication network for groups of similar trees in undisturbed woodland. When children see a ring of fungi, often called a tiger fairy ring, underneath the ground there is a vast mass producing the fruiting bodies (the toadstools), which are above the ground. We humans use a variety of fungi for our food production. Tell children about this when you come across foods such as yoghurt for example, and using one of the yeasts, a small unicellular fungus used in baking and brewing beer. Children may be familiar with the moulds that cover food that is 'off'. If you leave slices of moist bread out, a network of a fungus called *Rhyzopus stolonifer* will grow across the surface. If doing this in nursery or a non-home environment, put the moist bread in a see-through container with a cover just in case a child is allergic to spores.

The most common fungus of which children may be aware is probably an edible mushroom, often bought in tins as button mushrooms. These young mushrooms will have a covering underneath the cap, known as the veil, which covers the gills where the spores (which grow into new mushrooms) are found. In older edible mushrooms, which are much larger, the brown gills are exposed under the cap with the veil

58 Learning about plants

remaining as a ring of tissue around the stalk. Some people name all members of the group of fungi with the stem and cap as mushrooms. When shown a mushroom many young children in England recognise them – 'I eat them'. Young learners recognise mushrooms from seeing them in shops and at home where they were eaten. A 7-year-old boy justified his identification of the fungi he was shown as mushroom saying, 'I know because it's the shape, the top and the colour and my Mum cooks them!' Young children, as well as older ones, recognised the edible mushrooms shown to them because they were familiar with them from seeing them in shops and at home. Children were able to describe them. One child told me that mushrooms were white and grew on the ground. It has a certain shape like a crack all around underneath it. Another young child described mushrooms precisely as having a round bit on top, a stalk and definite 'mushroom' smell. When we interviewed English children from 4 years old to teenagers about mushrooms (Tunnicliffe, Boulter and Reiss, 2011), they did not refer to other fungi as mushrooms, only the edible ones. In the USA the term for fungi seems to be mushroom, but not in the UK, except in some everyday talk. There was no mention of Fly Agaric, the highly poisonous, scarlet-capped variety of fungi which is very often pictured in children's story books.

Conclusion

Plants are essential for other living things to exist, but they are often overlooked. Children associate fruits and vegetables as plants that may be eaten; seeds are associated with growing new plants that are wanted, yet they may hear plants described as 'weeds' by their parents and associate those with something unwanted or in the wrong place. Plants are green, they are immobile. Young children enjoy planting seeds and respond well to receiving assistance in exploring the botanical world. As with animals, children easily become familiar with their everyday names and are most familiar with the terms 'flowers' and 'trees'. The next chapter discusses how children start to name living things.

References

Allen, W. (2003) Plant blindness. *Bioscience*, 53(10): 926. DOI: 10.1641/0006-3568(2003)053 [0926:PB]2.0.CO;2.

Barker, J. (1995) A plant is an animal standing on its head. *Journal of Biological Education*, 29(3): 203–208.

Bartoszeck, A.B., Cosmo, C.R., da Silva, B.R. and Tunnicliffe, S.D. (2015) Concepts of plants held by young Brazilian children: an exploratory study. *European Journal of Educational Research*, 4(3): 105–117.

Braund, M. and Reiss, M. (eds). (2004) *Learning Science Outside the Classroom*. New York: Routledge Falmer.

Gatt, S., Tunnicliffe, S.D., Borg, K. and Lautie, K. (2007) Young Maltese children's ideas about plants. *Journal of Biological Education*, 41(3): 117–121.

Hadzigeorgiou, Y. (2015) Young children's ideas about physical science concepts. In Trundle, K.C. and Saçkes, M. (eds), *Research in Early Childhood Science*. Dordrecht: Springer, pp. 67–98.

Lindemann-Mathies, P. (2005) 'Loveable' mammals and 'lifeless' plants: how children's interest in common local organisms can be enhanced through observation of nature. *International Journal of Science Education*, 27(6): 655–677.

Lindemann-Mathies, P. (2006) Investigating nature on the way to school. *International Journal of Science Education*, 28(8): 895–918.

Louv, R. (2006) *Last Child in the Woods. Saving Our Children from Nature-Deficit Disorder.* Chapel Hill, NC: Algonquin Books.

Patrick, P. and Tunnicliffe, S.D. (2011) What plants and animals do early childhood and primary students name? Where do they see them? *Journal of Science and Educational Technology*, 20(5): 630–642.

Rybska, E., Sajkowska, Z.A. and Tunnicliffe, S.D. (2014) What's inside a tree? The ideas of five-year-old children. *Journal of Emergent Science*, 8: 7–15.

Rybska, E., Tunnicliffe, S.D. and Sajkowska, Z.A. (2016) Children's ideas about the internal structure of trees: cross-age studies. *Journal of Biological Education*, 51(4): 1–16. DOI: 10.1080/00219266.2016.1257500.

Sanders, D. and Jenkins, D. (2018) Plant biology. In Kampourakis, C. and Reiss, M.J. (eds), *Teaching Biology in Schools: Global Research Issues and Trends.* Abingdon, UK: Routledge, p. 125.

Sanders, D.L. (2007) Making public the private life of plants: the contribution of informal learning environments. *International Journal of Science Education*, 29(10): 1209–1228.

Schneekloth, L.H. (1989) Where did you go?' 'The forest.' 'What did you see?' 'Nothing'. *Children's Environmental Quarterly*, 6(1): 14–17.

Schreck Reiss, C., Moreira, A., Nunes, H., Azevedo, C., López, R. and Trincão, P. (2014) Botanic kits 'let's sow science!'. In Costa, M., Pombo, P., and Vazquez Dorrío, J. (eds), *Hands-on Science. Science Education with and for Society.* Braga: Hands-on Science Network, pp. 87–96.

Simard, S.W., Perry, D.A., Jones, M.D., Myrold, D.D., Durall, D.M. and Molina, R. (1997) Net transfer of carbon between ectomycorrhizal tree species in the field. *Nature*, 388(6642): 579.

Simmons, D. (1994) Urban children's preferences for nature: lessons for environmental education. *Children's Environments*, 11(3): 194–203.

Tavares, A.C. (2013) *A alga que queria ser flor.* Coimbra: Coimbra University Press.

Tunnicliffe, S. (2001) Talking about plants – comments of primary school groups looking at plants as exhibits in a botanical garden. *Journal of Biological Education*, 36(1): 27–34.

Tunnicliffe, S. (2013) *Talking and Doing Science in the Early Years: A Practical Guide for Ages 2–7.* London: Routledge, p. 15.

Tunnicliffe, S.D. (1999) What's inside a tree? *Primary Science and Technology Today*, (11): 3–5.

Tunnicliffe, S.D., Boulter, C. and Reiss, M.J. (2011) Getting children to talk about what they know of the natural world. *Primary Science*, 119: 24–26.

Tunnicliffe S.D. and Reiss M.J. (1999) Building a model of the environment: how do children see animals. *Journal of Biological Education*, 33(4): 142–148.

Tunnicliffe, S.D. and Reiss, M.J. (2000) Building a model of the environment: how do children see plants? *Journal of Biological Education*, 34: 172–177.

Tunnicliffe, S.D. and Reiss, M.J. (2001) 'What's inside bodies?'. Learning about skeletons and other organ systems of vertebrate animals. In Valanides, N. (ed), Proceedings of the 1st Symposium of the International Organisation for Science and Technology Education in Southern Europe. Paralimni, Cyprus: Imprinta, pp. 84–94.

Tunnicliffe, S.D. and Ueckert, C. (2011) Early biology: the critical years for learning biology. *Journal of Biological Education*, 45(4): 173–175.

Villaroel, J.D. (2015) Young children's drawings of plant life: a study concerning the use of colours and its relationship to age. *Journal of Biological Education*, 50(1): 41–53.

Wandersee, J.H. and Schussler, E.E. (1999) Preventing plant blindness. *The American Biology Teacher*, 61(2): 82–86.

Wohlleben, P. (2017) *The Hidden Life of Trees.* London: Collins.

Chapter 5

Observing changes in living things

Introduction

Young children have trouble with the idea of time. They become confused by changes that are not instant. When she was 4, Ellie planted a seed, covering it with 'soil' in a little pot. She placed it carefully outside and after a few hours returned to monitor its progress. Believing it to be a rapid process she returned to her grandma very upset because the seed had not yet grown. At the same age, Ellie and her sister made fairy cakes with their grandmother. They carefully mixed the ingredients, spooned it into paper cake cases and placed them in the oven. They could not believe that the cakes were not formed at once. Time again had to pass.

Young children notice grey hair in older people, they notice that older adults may move more slowly and do not engage in the same lively games as younger people do. Recently a colleague and I visited a school and a 5-year-old boy asked if my colleague was the teacher's grandmother because they both had white hair. The younger lady had very blonde hair and her face was much smoother! Age is often estimated by the appearance of physical attributes such as wrinkles and hair colour, but recognising the stages in the life history of other organisms is not always as easy; young children assume that smaller similar looking animals are the young of the larger animals. At a natural history diorama of an Angolan savannah, the main central feature was an adult, giant sable antelope (*Hippotragus niger*) standing on a termite mound with two smaller antelopes of a different species, the impala (*Aeplyceros melampus*). Children were of the opinion that the small animals were the young of the larger animal (Reiss and Tunnicliffe, 2012).

The stages from babyhood to adulthood

Children at different stages of development show a particular interest in specific content related to birth education. Young children gradually learn about the stages in the lives of organisms: pre-birth, birth, from very young to adult, and the ways in which plants and animals change gradually.

Talk science: life cycles

Ask why babies don't look like grown-ups? What happens? What babies have they seen? Where? Do these babies look like their mother or father?

The life cycle

Two adults are usually necessary so that a female sex cell can be fertilised by a male sex cell. After adults have reproduced they have completed their biological job. The life cycle of this organism continues but with new individuals each turn of the circle. The two sex cell producers must be of the same kind of living thing. One is called male and the other female.

From their earliest existence, which starts pre-birth with the seed developing in fruit on its parent plant or a developing animal in an egg or inside its mother's uterus. With flowering plants you can start with a fruit containing seeds, which contain the embryo (the baby plants in the form of the seed), such as a pea (*Pisum sativum*) or nasturtium (*Tropaeolum*) seed that is released from the fruit of the adult. The seed, if it has landed on a suitable growing medium, begins to grow. This is the young stage. The two cotyledons emerge from the ground and then the growing plant enters its change stage. The seedling begins to grow into the form of the adult plant. It grows a stem, with in some cases, depending on the type of plant, sideshoots. Leaves develop and buds may appear which contain the flowers. The adult form is when there are flowers; the old form is when there are fruits which dry up having released their seeds.

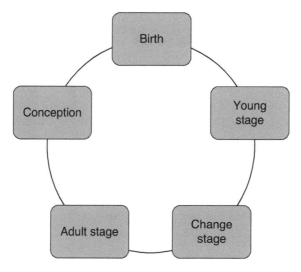

Figure 5.1 Life cycle summary
Source: The author

Biologically, as in all species, they have completed their 'job'. In plants that are biennials (that is, they live for two years) the process is repeated by the adult plant which comes up again the next year and dies after the second season. Biennials include foxgloves (*Digitalis pupurea*) and wallflowers (*Cheiranthus cheiri*). Children gradually learn about annuals, biennials and perennials and pointing out examples to them is very helpful. Collecting seeds, particularly those of nasturtiums and sowing them again early next year reinforces the annual life cycle. Some plants are called perennial; they live year after year, as many larger plants do that take many years to reach maturity when they can reproduce. Perennial plants, like mature trees and rose bushes, for example, continue to reproduce. Children enjoy the annual collection of the seeds of the horse chestnut tree (*Aesculus hippocastanum*) which are seen in the autumn. From September onwards young children collect the seeds, taking them out of the spiky fruit to play 'conkers'. Some herbaceous perennials die above ground but new shoots appear in the following spring. Bulbs such as daffodils also do this, although they do not necessarily flower the next year. The old stage is when the organism has lost the ability to reproduce (this stage in the female human is called menopause).

 Talk science: new life

Can a youngster explain the changes that occur in humans as they change from a baby to a grown up? How are they different now from when they were a baby? How are they different from their mother and father? What changes have occurred? What has stayed the same? How could you make a model to show the changes that happen from the baby of any species to the grown-up?

 Activity: looking inside seeds

Look closely at the fruits of a leguminous plant such as a pea pod, a runner bean, a broad bean or mange tout. Look at the outside of the pod. Can you see the outline of the seeds through the fruit? Open it and what do you notice? Where are the seeds? How are they attached to the pod? Is there a stalk attaching them? What have you found out? Are the seeds attached to the pod of their mother plant? Think about the following: does each pod of the same kind of plant have the same number of seeds? Count the number of seeds in one pod. Do all pods have the same number of seeds? Count the number of seeds in ten pods. Make a graph of your results.
What did you find? What did you learn? Were your predictions correct?

Activity: flowering plant life circles

This activity is to make a life circle and reinforce the stages in various species. You will need two card circles, a paper fastener and pictures of the various stages. Divide one of the card circles into five equal segments. Divide the top piece of card likewise. Cut out one of the segments leaving a piece of card around the centre for strength. Label each segment, 1= pre-birth, 2 = birth, 3 = young, 4 = change, 5 = adult stage. Fix on the top circle and turn it to show the sequence. This activity can be varied to make cards which must be sequenced or a board game where the card is picked up to fill in a strip or life circle.

 Activity: a life circle for older children

Cut out two circular pieces of card of the same size and divide each into five equal segments. Label each segment with the name of different stages of the life circles of a plant from seed to seedling to plant to adult with flowers making seeds, then the fruits and seed release (or cones in the case of conifers that have cones not flowers) with their seeds. Place one circle on top of the other, cut out one segment of the upper circle and fix it in the middle with a split pin, and illustrate the progression of change of forms in a life cycle using the circle. Alternatively, you can make a 3D circle inside a hoop or make a ring of hoops (or metal coat hangers pulled out into a square shape), or chalk the circles on a washable surface, placing a living representative of each stage inside the relevant life stage of the hoop. Divisions between stages can be made by pieces of tape or string attached to a card circle in the middle of the hoop! It is fun and invites children of all ages to collaborate.

Metamorphosis – the change as an organism grows from baby to adult

Many young plants or animals look different when they are babies. All babies change to the adult form. This changing is called metamorphosis. If the young form does not exactly resemble the adult, young children may assume that the two differing forms are different species. Bruner, Goodnow and Austin (1956) recognised this as an issue in the understanding of the diverse forms of animals with complete metamorphosis and their relationship to each other. These are the phenomena of inclusion and exclusion. Children, as do adults, notice different stages of an animal within the life cycle of the species, e.g. caterpillar, pupa and imago of a butterfly; tadpole and amphibian. In plants, children require additional guidance in learning the stages of growth. Consider the following topics for discussion and plan appropriate activities that will encourage them to think about growth and development in plants.

64 Observing changes in living things

 Talk science: young plants

What do your learners know about young plants? Do baby plants look like the grown flowering plants? What do they think? Why do they think that? Can they tell from a seedling what kind of plant it will grow up to be?

 Activity: getting to know seedlings

Grow or obtain trays of seedlings. Rape and cress seeds can be bought at grocery stores and supermarkets. Other seedlings can be bought at garden centres or young saplings found at the base of older trees. Look for young plants with green leaves but no flowers. Alternatively, you can grow sprouting seeds in a jar or, if you buy a packet of seeds of a flowering plant, keep the seed packet with a picture of the plant in flower.

 Talk science: lookalikes?

Ask: do young plants look like the grown-up plants or not? What is similar? What is different? Is an adult plant bigger than the baby plants? If so, by how much? How can they tell it is a flowering herbaceous plant? What changes for it to be considered grown-up?

 Activity: young trees, old trees

Can they work out if a tree is old and, if so, what are the signs that cause them to think it is old? What time of the year do you expect to see flowers? What colours are the first flowers of the year? When do some trees lose their leaves and when do leaves appear again? What tells the children that the leaves are old?

Growing from a seed to an adult plant

Children learn quickly that seeds will turn into plants – they need to be planted in soil and watered to help them grow.

> **Talk science: what plants need to grow**
>
> Ask: what does a plant need to grow? Why do they think that?
> Where did they find that out? What do they need to grow as a young human?
> Do they need the same things as plants?

One-parent babies

Vegetative reproduction by one parent only or a solo parent (mother) can occur in some plant species where the two parents are not needed. Some plants root easily from cuttings grown in water, and when large enough, may be planted out or 'potted on'.

Young stems of forsythia (*Forsythia spectabilis*) or willow (*Salix caprea*), commonly called goat willow or pussy willow, root like this easily. Spider plants (*Chlorophytum comosum*) are often seen in schools or households and grow stems sideways, on which small plantlets develop. The same process happens in strawberry plants and blackberries. Bulbs produce smaller bulbils under the ground – snowdrops, when dug up carefully while 'in the green', display the bulbs beneath the flowering stems and similarly, crocus corms produce smaller corms on top of each other. Children find it exciting to excavate these treasures from potted plants, pushing aside the compost to see the new baby bulbs.

Meet the seeds!

Seeds are young flowering plants enclosed in a protective coat. Seeds are developed in the ovary or 'egg box' of flowering plants; in the middle, inside the ring of male parts (or stamens) and they usually develop after fertilisation. This is at the bottom of the female sex organs. The seeds have one- or two-seed leaves (*cotyledons*) depending on which type of flowering plant they are. The point where the seed was attached to the mother plant in the ovary is called the hilum and can be seen easily on a Mung or French bean. This is scar of the attachment stalk from the seed to the mother plant through which the seed obtained its food whilst inside the seed, just as baby mammals obtain their food inside their mother's uterus through the umbilical cord.

The root is called the *radicle* and can be seen through the skin or *testa* in a special pocket above the hilum and micropyle. If the seed coat is removed from a French bean two seed leaves or *cotyledons* are revealed with the baby plant or *embryo* in between them. The radicle is one end of the embryo and the two seed leaves are joined by a stalk. Flowering plants are the most familiar plants, but they contain trees and shrubs as well as pot plants, wild flowers and bedding plants. Flowering plants can be divided into those with one seed leaf, called *monocotyledons* (*mono* = one cotyledon is seed leaf and food store for developing baby plant until it can use sunlight to produce its own food), which have parallel lines on their leaves like a tulip, daffodil or grass leaf, and *dicotyledons* (*di* = two cotyledons), which have branched patterns of veins on their leaves like a rose or geranium. They have two seed leaves in their seed, as seen in pea or bean seeds, whereas if a sweetcorn seed is examined only one seed leaf will be found.

Seeds need to absorb water before they grow. They also need oxygen and a suitable temperature. The first sign of growth after the seed has been planted is the root bursting through the seed coat. Whichever way up this has been planted the root grows downwards and the shoot grows upwards. The young plant uses up the food in its seed leaves until either they or new leaves, in turn, grow above ground and start making food using the energy of the sun in the process called photosynthesis.

 Talk science: seeds need water

Have you ever grown a seed or seen someone do that? What do seeds look like before they start growing, have you ever seen seeds come from a flowering plant or from a packet? If so what were they like? What had to happen to them before they were planted so they weren't dry and wrinkled? What do the emergent scientists think?

Leaving the mother plant: fruit and seed dispersal

Fruits and seeds are spread by:

Wind, e.g. dandelion fruits, poppy seeds or ash keys shaken out of their capsule as the wind blows.
Animals, e.g. goose grass, which clings to animals or berries the animal has eaten which pass out with the animal's droppings, or humans who plant seeds in their gardens.
Water, where the fruits and seeds are carried away, e.g. coconut.
Explosive ways, where the seeds are propelled from the fruit, e.g. Broom (*Cytisus striatus*) or Bizzie Lizzie (*Impatiens walleriana*).

All living things grow; this is part of being alive. Living things start very small – we humans begin as the size of a full stop. Living things begin by growing inside their mother. Plants leave their parent as a seed which contains the embryo, or baby, and a food store to last the plant until it has grown its own green leaves or until its special seed leaves grow above the ground and can make food until the true leaves have developed and take over this role, e.g. mustard seeds. The seeds lie dormant in the soil during the winter and begin to grow (germinate), when conditions are suitable in the spring when the earth begins to warm up.

When the seed leaves (cotyledons) emerge above ground they form the first leaves which make food, this is called epigeal germination. When the seed leaves or cotyledons stay beneath the ground so the plant grows its first real leaves above the ground which then photosynthesise, the germination is referred to as hypogeal (hypo = below). Plants which have one seed leaf (monocotyledons) have parallel lines called veins on their leaves, like grass, and those with two are called dicotyledons. They usually have reticulate branching on their leaves, e.g. French beans or roses.

Talk science: why do plants make seeds?

Producing seeds is what flowering plants do. Have the children ever seen plants with fruits and seeds? When are seeds distributed into the air by plants? Do they know when?

Requirements for growth

Plants require certain conditions to grow: air, light, mineral salts and water, as well as a little wind, adequate soil and protection from damage, including from other animals or plants which compete for the same requirements and which, in some cases, overgrow the plant and choke it (e.g. bindweed). The oldest living things in the world are bristle cone pines which may be found in the Mojave desert in North America and the largest living thing in the world is the giant redwood, or sequoia, which is found in the Sequoia National Park in California.

Seeds are easy to investigate. If you ask children if they like peas or baked beans for example, talk about why they eat them. Where do they think these food beans are made before they are canned? Explain that all animals rely on plants for their energy, even if the animal does not directly eat the ants, the animal that the animal eats has done. This is known as a food chain. These are vital for the seed for they are the food supply for the baby plant provided by the mother plant. Who provides some food for you?

A popular activity for children who have some manipulative skill is to 'Give birth to a sweet corn' (by pressing in the white part of the corn, the embryo pops out). The sweetcorn is from a type of maize plant, its fruit is a small kernel and inside is the food store and the embryo. Kernels produced on the large cob are often covered with papery-like green covers from the flower spike of the adult plant.

Talk science: leaving its seed

Ask children what fruits they know. What is the difference between a very young one and an old one, for example an apple? What is inside a fruit, for example an apple, an orange or a melon?

Parental care in flowering plants

Looking after babies before they are born is something all living things do in some way. Children are frequently fascinated by looking inside the fruits and vegetables we buy to identify the seeds in the pod, whose role is to protect the embryo and feed it, like that of the mammalian placenta or the shell of a bird's egg. Open the pods of mangetout or broad beans and examine the stalks that connect the seed to the wall of the fruit (the pod). This is how the seed obtains its food until it is big enough to leave the parent and live by itself. This is parental care, just as it is in mammals, where the placenta feeds the developing baby inside the mother's uterus.

Talk science: how do seeds grow?

Have you ever grown a seed? Can you grow a seed? Would you like to? What shall we do? What do you think? Which seed would you choose?

Activity: how to grow seeds

Ask the children what they think they need to grow a seed and why. Let them plant their seed. Watch what happens each day.

Talk science: wrinkly seeds

Children have sometimes asked why the seeds in a packet don't grow in the packet. What are their ideas? How could you help them to find out?

Activity: wrinkly seeds

Seeds need water to start to grow! Place a few dry seeds – chick peas or broad beans are excellent for this – onto small dishes. Put water in one of the dishes and leave the other dry. What do the children think will happen? Why do they think that? Wait 24 hours. What do you see? One seed usually soaks up the water and loses it wrinkles and its dry, hard feel. What happens if you continue watching over several days? What does the child notice?

Observing changes in living things 69

Growing up as a plant

All living things have to grow from birth to independent life and adulthood when they feed themselves, find their own place to live and mate. Some new living things, calves and foals, for example, are able to do this as soon as they leave the mother while others, like human babies, cannot.

Talk science: care or no care?

Talk about which plants and animals look after themselves once they are born and which need looking after? Is there a pattern? A general rule? How do living things that have no aftercare from the parent manage to find food and grow? What do you think? Why? What is your evidence? What are your examples?

Activity: getting to know seeds

You need a card with one of each of the four seeds (listed in Table 5.1) attached by clear adhesive tape or glue; cotton wool buds; a small pot of water, which may be useful for moving some of the seeds – especially the marigold and the mustard, which are tiny; a piece of kitchen towel or 1 cm squared paper on which to place the seeds to examine them; rulers; pieces of string/wool about 10 cm in length to use for measuring; and copies of the charts in which they can record their observations (see Table 5.1). Ask the children whether they have drawn the seeds the actual size, bigger than actual size or smaller than actual size. If they have drawn the seeds bigger, ask them how many times bigger. Similarly, if they have drawn the seeds smaller, which is unlikely, ask them how many times smaller their drawing is than the actual seeds.

Table 5.1 Seed length, colour and shape

Seed Name	Drawing	Length	Colour	Shape
French bean				
Mustard				
Marigold				
Mung bean				

Ask the children to find out about the seeds in terms of:

1. Their length.
2. Their colour.
3. Their shape.

Talk about what they have found out and come to a consensus. You could compile a 'master' chart on a piece of sugar paper, a whiteboard or a chalkboard. This could be useful to refer to in the next activity.

Activity: which is which?

This activity consolidates the observations which the children have made in the previous activity and provides practice in grouping and making and using keys.

Try to draw a YES/NO key to group the seeds so that someone who does not know their individual names can identify them. Make a branch key for each of the criteria described in the previous activity. This can be worked out on a tablet or computer once a learner has mastered the technique and thought it through. Below, in Figures 5.2, 5.3 and 5.4, are examples of three simple branch keys to distinguish between three kinds of seed: a marigold seed, Mung bean and a French bean, by looking at three different characteristics.

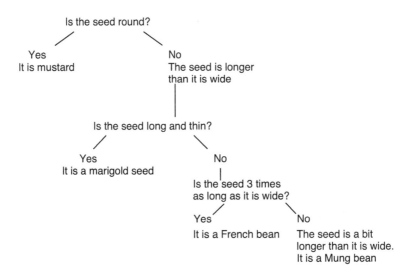

Figure 5.2 Key 1 – shape key
Source: The author

Observing changes in living things 71

Figure 5.3 Key 2 – colour key
Source: The author

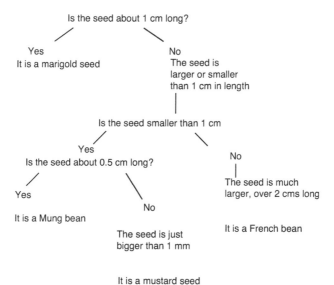

Figure 5.4 Key 3 – size key
Source: The author

If your child is not yet skilled in using standard measurements, use non-standard ones such as a counter or fingernail length. You can use pieces of wool to make the actual measurement and then lay the wool on a ruler and read off the measurement.

You could also use the size of squares on squared paper as a measure. As an extension task, give the children other easily obtainable seeds – sunflower, peas and broad beans for example, and ask them to construct keys for these 'new' seeds.

 Activity: plant babies

You need mangetout or runner bean pods (frozen packs are useful out of season), a dish, a hand lens or other magnifier. Examine the pods and see if the remains of the parts of the flower can be seen. Draw the pod (put the size, e.g. x 1 for life size). Split open the fruit. Find the seeds. How are they arranged? How are they fixed to the mother? There should be a stalk that attaches the seed (the scar form of this is called the *hilum*) to the placenta. This stalk is like the umbilical cord of a mammal.

 Activity: inside a bean

You need soaked French beans, pots and paper towels. Give a bean to each child or group of two. Ask the children to identify the external parts. They should find the *hilum* and *micropyle*. Ask them to remove the seed coat. What do they find? They should be able to see the embryo, the seed leaf stalk and the two seed leaves (which means this is a dicotyledonous seed). Try looking, using a hand lens, at the Mung bean. Is the structure similar or different? Introduce some other seeds like sweetcorn and sunflowers. What do the children find?

 Activity: seeds and water

You need: 40 dry Mung beans per group, measuring scales, pots or plastic beakers of equal size, syringes for measuring water and paper towels. The children should divide the seeds into two piles of dry Mung beans of equal weight. Thereafter, the only differences in weight must be due to other factors. Put the seeds into two containers. Add enough water so that the beans are just covered. Record the volume of water. What do the children think will happen? Record their predictions. How is this a fair test? Design and make a record chart, perhaps like that shown in Table 5.2.

Observing changes in living things 73

Table 5.2 Tracking absorption of water by seeds

Names:			
Time and date	Seeds with water	Seeds without water	My explanation

When the seeds have absorbed their water, encourage the more able children to work out approximately how much water the 20 Mung beans have soaked up and then work out how much a single Mung bean has absorbed.

 Talk science: why seeds?

Why do flowering plants make seeds? What happens to a seed? Does it change ever? Why are seeds there? What does a young scientist think? Why do they think that?

 Activity: grow root! GROW!

You need a seed that has been soaked in water and a see-through pot, e.g, a plastic beaker, with a piece of paper towel to fill the inside. Place the seed between the wall of the pot and the kitchen towel. Watch what happens each day and talk about what is happening and why.

 Activity: grow a seed!

Add a few mls of water to the pot so the paper is just damp. Place several different kinds of seeds outside the paper so they are visible next to the sides of the pot. Leave the pot and watch what happens. Keep an observation diary and draw each seed each day. Which bit will come out of the seed first? It is expected that the root will sprout first. The shoot appears second and, whichever way up the seed was 'planted' the root will grow downwards. After some days root hairs will appear

74 Observing changes in living things

just behind the tip of the root. This is very noticeable in the Mung beans. Side roots will develop after about five days in the French bean. The roots take in water and other nutrients for the plants and keep the plant anchored in the ground. Not all roots are like those in beans. Carrots and beetroot, for example, have a thick tap root. Keep a chart (Table 5.3) of your observations and of how your seed develops.

Table 5.3 Observations of a growing seed

Name	Seed	Day 'planted'	
Day 1	Drawing	Other observations	What I think is happening

 Activity: upside down and in the way

You need the same items as in the previous activity, plus a stone or something to use to put in the way of the root. Each group should plant two more soaked seeds, each in a separate pot. Label one 'UPSIDE DOWN' and the other 'ROOT OBSTRUCTION'. Plant one upside down. Plant the other the correct way but put something in the way of the path of the root to investigate what happens when the root meets an obstruction. Use copies of the chart from the previous activity for each seed.

 Activity: where are the seeds?

Collect a variety of fruits, e.g. peas, apples, oranges, marrows, tomatos, bananas, courgettes (zucchini) or cucumber, pomegranates, plums, prunes or dates. Ask the children where they can find the seeds? The adult can open the fruits with a knife to show them.

 Activity: getting away!

You need ash or sycamore keys if possible, or a winged fruit (if not a picture of them). Ask the children how the keys move through the air and see if they can make a paper helicopter that has the same action using the following instructions. You will need a piece of A4 paper, a pair of scissors and a paperclip.

1) Take the piece of A4 paper and fold it in half lengthways.
2) Cut along the fold and then fold one of the pieces in half lengthways again.
3) Fold the paper lengthways for a third time then unfold it so that you can see the crease made by this fold along the paper.
4) Now fold the piece of paper widthways, then again unfold so the crease can be seen.
5) Cut along the long crease on one side, stopping about 2.5cm before the middle point created by the folds.
6) Next cut along each of the small creases (so along the width of the rectangle), this time stopping about 1.5cm from the middle point on each side.
7) Working with the half of the rectangle that has not been cut, fold the top quarter of the rectangle in half lengthways and then do the same with the other side. The folded edges of these should meet in the middle.
8) Fold the whole rectangle in half, again lengthways, along the crease already made. The two flaps made in the previous step should now be face to face. Secure them at the bottom with the paperclip.
9) Finally, fold the remaining two quarters of the rectangle out so that the paper resembles a 'T' shape.
10) Drop the paper helicopter from a height with the paperclip at the bottom.

 Activity: seed collages

Using the seeds (or those which can be bought in the shops, e.g. rice, sunflowers, dried peas) make a seed collage.

 Activity: do seeds need water?

You need: some dried seeds (e.g. Mung beans),* two tubs, kitchen towel scrunched up at the bottom of the tubs, some water and a measuring jug.

*You may prefer to wash the Mung beans first and re-dry them because green colourant comes off the seed coat. You can use the French beans but the Mung beans sprout within 24 hours.

Count out the same number of beans into each tub, e.g. five beans.

To one tub add some water, e.g. 10 ml, so that the paper towel is completely wet.

Leave the peas and observe them every day. What happens? Have the children design an observation chart to fill in at regular intervals. Can they explain their observations?

Expected outcome: that the dry beans will not sprout and will remain the same size whilst the peas with water will a) swell up and b) sprout.

76 Observing changes in living things

 Activity: how much water do seeds take in?

You need:

40 dried Mung beans (10 if using French beans).
Weighing scales.
Water in measuring beaker and a syringe.
A pot large enough to hold the beans.
Paper towel.

Weigh a) one of the pots and b) the beans within the pot. Make note of all the weights measured then work out the weight of the beans alone, followed by the average weight of one bean as follows:

Weight of beans = total weight of beans and pot − weight of pot (refer to this value as weight A).

Average weight of one bean (weight B) = weight of beans (weight A)/40.

Add 10 ml of water to the beans in the pot using the syringe. If all the water disappears add another 5 ml. Repeat this until the water no longer disappears. Write down the total amount of water added to the pot of beans.

After 24 hours weigh the beans again in their pot. If there is any water at the bottom of the pot that has not been absorbed, soak this up with a paper towel before weighing them. Take weight A (the weight of the dried beans and pot away from this weight, which is the weight of the wet beans and pot). The answer gives the weight of water that has been soaked up by the 40 beans. Now divide this value by 40 to find the average weight of one soaked Mung bean. Compare this with weight B. How much water has each bean absorbed?

 Activity: cold and warm

You need six French beans that have been soaked in water, six identically sized pots, damp paper towel, a refrigerator (or very cold place) and a thermometer which measures outside temperatures. Make up six pots of beans and put two in the cold place, leave two in the room and put two somewhere warm. Record the temperatures of the three sites. Watch the beans each day and keep a record of what happens to them. Keep the observations in a table, similar to the one suggested in Table 5.4.

Table 5.4 Comparison of growing seeds in warm and cold environments

Day	Cold site °C	Room temperature °C	Warm site temp °C

The expected outcome is that the beans kept at room temperature and in the warm room will germinate (sprout).

Observing changes in living things 77

 Activity: moving to the light – seedlings

You need scissors, a shoe box with a lid and a slit (5 cm × 6cm) at one end through which light can get into the box, mustard seeds and small containers for the seeds. Grow some mustard seedlings, all of which are growing up straight, and put some in a small low-sided container so there are two pots of seedlings. Alternatively, you can buy a box of seedlings from the supermarket and divide the seedlings into two halves. Place each group of seedlings in a separate dish. Place one pot in the dark box and place the others on a table in the room with light all around it. Watch the seedlings. After four days, what has happened? The expected outcome will be that the seedlings with the light coming at them from the slit in the box will have grown towards the light source, whereas the seedlings with the light all around them will have continued growing straight up. Is that what you expected. Why?

Animal change

Many children's picture books feature developing organisms such as seeds growing into flowers, tadpoles changing into frogs or caterpillars changing to butterflies so young children may possess some knowledge, however, their understanding is frequently inaccurate.

Observing change in animal life poses problems for the indoor learning environment. Tadpoles are difficult to keep. During the change stage they are carnivorous, not vegetarian. They need meat and will eat each other if no other source is available. Remember too, that in the UK, it is illegal to collect them from the wild (CLEAPSS, 2005). However, the mealworm, *Tenebrio molitor*, is ideal. It clearly shows the distinct stages of its complete change, or metamorphosis, from larva (often mistakenly called a maggot) to the adult. It changes its form completely. The mealworm larvae, white organisms about 2.5 cm or longer turn into a pupa, a white chocolate colour which appear very different. The organisms in a state of inertness gradually turn dark brown and shiny with a segmented appearance. From this emerges a small brown beetle – the adult is smaller than the larva at about 1.5 cm long. I have kept them most successfully and occasionally they mate and produce offspring. The eggs are too small to see with the naked eye. In the wild, these eggs are eaten by other animals. In school or elsewhere where they are kept, the animals can only thrive in the container. The containers will require cleaning once in a while as the excretory products build up, producing an odour.

The benefits of keeping animals in classrooms have long been recognised. Possible hazards are identified by CLEAPSS (Consortium of Local Education Authorities for the Provision of Science Services) (2005). CLEAPSS publications also advise on regulations and prohibitions on the safe keeping of animals.

Examining live organisms for themselves motivates pupils and renders teaching more effective, as well as engendering concern for those organisms (Cassidy and Tranter, 1996) – a concern which may be developed for other species and environmental issues. I have always maintained that working with mealworms provides opportunities for first-hand observations and thus, children's interpretations of structure and behaviours, while at the same time developing and using the scientific skills, such as the factual knowledge, processes and general skills such as problem solving, critical thinking, logistics of science investigations, and team work and collaboration (Tunnicliffe, 2016).

Activity: moving!

The investigation focused on movement in plants may also be carried out using small invertebrates. Very often primary/elementary schools use snails or woodlice, collected from outside. Sadly, in some instances, these organisms are not returned to their habitat or may be kept in unsuitable conditions and die. Children who have the opportunity to look outside may notice that some small organisms can be seen in dark, moist places. Ask them what they have noticed. Where would they go to look for woodlice, snails, centipedes and slugs? Mealworm larvae, however, respond ideally to investigation in the classroom. You need a tray that can be covered at one end so it is dark. Mealworms will move away from the light, they live, after all, in flour and grains. I keep mine in bran or oats. They will move towards moisture at one end of a tray.

Talk science: animal life circles

Can the emergent scientist talk about the changes from baby to adult in some animals? Does the baby animal always look like its biological parents, so you know what it will grow up to be, e.g. a kitten or a lamb? Or does the baby look very different to the adult it will become, e.g. an egg or a caterpillar?

Activity: animal life circles

You can make an individual life circle by obtaining and placing two card circles of identical size, and both divided into five equally-sized segments, one on top of the other. On the lower circle use stamps to put pictures of a life history, such as that of a frog, with eggs, tadpole with external gills at their 'young' stage, a tadpole with gills covered and back legs showing as the 'change' stage and a froglet as an 'adult'. You can also do this with butterflies or moths, with the change stage being the chrysalis or cocoon, or mealworms where the change stage is a pupa. Some children enjoy finding or drawing pictures of human life stages to illustrate their life circle or that of a domestic animal such as a kitten.

Changes as new life grows

Change in plants and animals begin before birth, with the development of the fertilised egg. Using the term 'new life' encompasses all births, starting life from the fertilised egg, and development, in all plants and animals. However, 'sex education' is an emotive term and 'new life' is not. When used it includes the biology of creating new organisms and is concerned with necessary behaviours of the two components of sexual reproduction and the subsequent formation of a new organism, which is not concerned with relationships, human practice and customs. This, instead, is biological science. The basic ideas can be taught if necessary, entirely through reference to plants, the ideas and action are the same as for animals. I have taught in this way as necessary, depending on the ethos of the school (Tunnicliffe, 2010).

'An animal is an animal if it has babies', is a comment made by several young children, but how and where those babies are made is a mystery. Ideas soon emerge from the child's observations, experiences and from overhearing adults and older children talk.

When I taught antenatal classes I had many books about human and animal babies which parents borrowed to share with their other children. A mother once returned a sad-looking book rather apologetically — her toddler daughter had planted the book in the garden so it could grow the baby. She had made the connection between planting seeds and growing new plants and assumed that is what you did to grow the baby. Sometimes parents wanted to demonstrate how the baby grew in size — this can be done with the following, in size order: a full stop, dried pea, a 1p coin, a 5p coin, a 50p piece, a walnut and a grapefruit (which is about the size of a baby at 12 weeks from conception).

Occasionally parents and teachers would explain the baby being fed inside its mother by attaching a bath sponge to one end of a pyjama cord and then taping the other end of the cord to a baby doll's 'umbilicus' within a polythene bag to represent the membranes around the mammalian baby.

Young children learn through observation and comments that human babies come from a bulge at the front of the body. Many children replicate the first bulge by stuffing a cushion, teddy bear or doll beneath their pullovers so that they can 'have a baby too'.

Children are intrigued by babies, particularly human ones as the children approach puberty. A class of English 8-year-olds were invited to write down their questions about being a parent, being pregnant and looking after babies, as well as what interested the baby and its routine, and posted them in a box. Some parents had offered to visit the school with their babies and the children could address their questions directly to them, which the parents had seen in advance. The children were interested in the details of a baby's behaviour and development as well as the impact of its arrival on the parents. There were distinct gender differences in those topics, with some of particular interest to boys and others to girls. The English 8-year-old boys wanted to know information such as, 'When was the baby's birthday?' 'When does it sleep?' 'How heavy was it when it was born and how heavy is it now', whereas the girls were more interested in feelings about being a mother (Tunnicliffe, 2000).

Learning about new life in the early years

Interest in pregnancy and birth shown by children changes as they develop. This section is in two parts. Primary schools in England are not required to teach sex education to pre-secondary children in local authority schools. The Children and Social Work Act 2017 placed a duty on the Secretary of State for Education to make relationship education statutory in primary schools. New life education is biology, it is learning about the living world and forms a sound basis for future sex and relationship education in humans. Whilst sex education teaching in UK schools differs in detail according to the counties making up the UK, it is often about the biology of human reproduction and not relationships and other related issues such as emotions and pornography (Birmingham, 2018).

There are distinct phases in what young children are interested in. They have been defined from observation as follows:

Interest in new life

STAGE ONE: ENVIRONMENTAL AWARENESS, 0–2 years

Patterns: Using pictures or models, show representatives of the group being discussed, e.g. some toy cars, pebbles, models of several animals and plants to show living/non-living, examples of mother animals and their babies, e.g. a cow and calf. Groups looked at could include: living/non-living, plants, animals, mummies/daddies, babies/adults.

STAGE TWO: NATURAL HISTORY STAGE, 2–5 years (Play group/ nursery)

Difference between males/females, matching babies to adult forms. Species constancy. Special places for growing babies in all kinds. Fruits and seeds, flowers, range of animals.

STAGE THREE: LIFE CIRCLES 5–7 years (Key Stage 1 Infants)

Stages in the lives of organisms: pre-birth, birth, young, change, adult. Ways in which plants and animals change, gradual, e.g. humans, or complete metamorphosis, e.g. caterpillars and tadpoles. Sex cells meeting – pollination, babies leaving parent, fruits, seeds, frog spawn etc.

STAGE FOUR: BABIES 7–9 years (Lower juniors)

Babies of all species. Where babies come from. Pre-birth care, post-birth care, form, foetal growth, parental care. Abilities. Themselves as babies, examples of baby things such as pushchairs, nappies, toys etc.

STAGE FIVE: FACTS STAGE (PRE-ADOLESCENT) 9–11 (Upper juniors)

Making babies – sex cells meeting, pollination, copulation. Basic genetics. Stages of human labour. Techniques and technology. Changes at human puberty, menstruation etc.

STAGE SIX: ADOLESCENT STAGE 12–16 (Secondary school)

Learning about relationships, relating birth to the self. Child care. More detail of birth facts.

(Tunnicliffe, 2000)

Observing changes in living things 81

New life: making babies in the living world

There are several kinds of ways of making babies, the next generation of a species, in the living world, but basically the needs are the same if the offspring are going to vary in form from their parents. This mixing of features of the parents is essential if species are to adapt to changing conditions. Species change with time and this is the process of evolution. Mixing up the characteristics of the two parts of the parents, mating, is a word and a topic that children begin to find embarrassing at times, but about which they are curious; possibly because of the overwhelming interest in the subject as allied to humans in their society. It is, in my experience, easier to introduce the facts of these ways of bringing changes, the mating, through talking about flowering plants, pollination and so on, or other animals such as butterflies or pets.

Organisms reproduce to make more of their own kind and this requires individuals with certain characteristics; we name them male and female. The cells of all species contain many chemicals but the chromosomes, which are in pairs joined at their centres, contain the instructional sequences of four proteins which are arranged for building new individuals. The number of chromosomes possessed by a species differs from species to species, and normally remains constant within the species. Humans have 23 pairs, fruit flies have eight pairs. Two individuals exchanging characteristics must each give their characteristics to another organism like them. They do this by giving one half of their instructions (which come in two strands called chromosomes) to the other individual, so they each then have two strands again, but no longer identical. These two new strands join up to form a new baby when half a chromosome from a chromosome pair meet at fertilisation. The female ones are in the egg (along with food waiting to feed the developing baby), which is waiting for the male sex cell to reach it by whichever transport mechanisms that kind of living thing has developed. The male ones are in a motile cell, the sperms, which contain whole sets of male instructions that merge with the half set of the female's instructions so a new individual is formed. This now contains instructions with one half from the male and one half from the female to ensure the number of characteristics of that species is maintained.

 Activity: match babies to the mother and father with model animals

Match babies to the mother and father with model animals. What are the names for the mothers and babies, for example, the mother sheep is a ewe, the father sheep is a ram and the baby is the lamb.

Biological life-sized models may be borrowed from teachers' centres or from a secondary school. Health education units may have these models associated with human body organs as well as pregnancy and birth. The life-sized adult models of the human body are available in the two sexes so a child can see the differences between the adult human form. Once the position of the uterus has been established, the life-sized models of the development of pregnancy can be used. The baby is removable in all but the earliest model so it can be felt and discussed. Models of the birth process are also available.

Protecting developing mammalian babies before birth

Developing eggs of animals are full of nutrients and are sought after as food by other animals. Birds have what is called an amniotic egg, essentially a 'private pond', for each developing baby in a protective covering, the shell. Oxygen passes through the shell to the fluid inside which contains the developing bird. Hens' eggs, which are a staple food for many humans, do *not* contain a developing bird, but do contain all the nutrients for the growing baby bird had the egg been fertilised.

You can see the yolk if you break open a hen's egg into a dish. It is surrounded by yellowish fluid, the amnion and the yolk is held steady by two twists of white material either side. There is an air space at one end of the shell between two membranes enclosing the fluid and the yolk.

This egg leaves the mother's body before the baby develops. Birds are warm blooded, so usually the mother sits on the egg to keep it warm until the chick hatches. A chick has a 'tooth' on its beak which enables it to break its shell and get out of the shell when ready to hatch, or 'be born'. Developing baby mammals, however, stay in the membranes and fluid inside the mother's special place for babies, the uterus, where the baby is fed through a tube containing 'food' from her food whose nutrients are passed into her blood stream. The tube feeding the baby is called the umbilical cord and leads from the mother to her uterus. Instead of yolk, mammalian babies obtain their food from their mother's blood supply, just as her body does. The organ between mother and baby is called the placenta and is attached to the muscular wall of the uterus and to the mother's blood supply, to which the placenta interfaces through special connections with the wall of the uterus.

All mammals begin life in the amniotic fluid (or 'the waters'). The role of this amniotic fluid is to protect the baby, acting as a shock absorber to support the baby and maintain a constant temperature around it. The volume of water increases as the baby grows until several weeks before birth when it decreases. The fluid leaves the mother when the baby is born, the 'sac' is broken and the fluid rushes out. This is called 'the breaking of the waters' and is sometimes the first indication of labour. Thus, all mammals are wet when they are born.

Everyone begins life the size of a full stop. In the early weeks of pregnancy human babies resemble the unborn babies of other vertebrates. Humans grow more rapidly before birth than they do afterwards. In 38 weeks, they grow from the size of the full stop to their birth weight and size.

Once a fertilised egg is attached to the wall of the uterus the developing baby is called an embryo. At about nine weeks from conception the unborn baby looks distinctly human. It is then called a foetus. The developing baby grows bigger and bigger, longer and heavier until it is ready to be born and live outside of its mother, but it still cannot survive by itself and needs feeding and keeping warm for many months.

 Talk science: how much do human babies weigh?

Do the children know how much a human baby weighs? Do they know much they weigh now? What has happened to the baby's weight? What size do they think a baby is the minute it is made after the two baby making cells meet? How does this little egg grow into a full-size baby?

Observing changes in living things   83

 Activity: how big is a baby?

These are the average sizes of a developing baby during pregnancy:

At two weeks from conception the baby is the size of a full stop.
At six weeks it is the size of a dried pea and would fit on a 1p coin.
At seven weeks it fits on a 5p coin.
At eight weeks from conception the embryo is the size of a broad bean or an adult thumbnail, it covers a 50p coin. In the amniotic sac it is the size of a walnut.
At 14 weeks from conception the foetus is the length of an adult hand and the size of a grapefruit.

Collect one of each of the items listed above and use them to show the children how developing babies increase in size.

 Activity: how long is a baby?

Measure out strips of thin card equivalent to the lengths of the baby, as given in Table 5.5. Arrange them on a piece of large paper to make a bar chart. Label the Y-axis (up the side) as length and the X-axis (along the bottom) weeks of development. What do the children say about the length increase? Does it increase at the same rate over the weeks of development or does the rate increase, decrease or stay the same at certain points of development? The increasing length of the developing baby and the weeks of development are shown in Table 5.5.

Table 5.5 Length of foetus during pregnancy

Weeks of growing before birth	Length cm
4 weeks	Foetus 8 mm diameter
6 weeks	2.5 cm
12 weeks	8 cm
16 weeks	14 cm
18 weeks	16 cm
26 weeks	25 cm
30 weeks	30 cm
38 weeks (term) (40 weeks from last period)	35 cm

Finding a mate

Most plants do not move around from place to place to find a mate and making new life requires two half sets of chromosomes to meet. How do children think this can be solved? Do they know of examples of plants achieving this? Do they understand that all life on Earth depends on plants? Without plants there is no life.

Seed making plants, including conifers and flowering plants, have evolved mechanisms for the half sets to meet. They produce pollen, which has the male set of chromosomes, and have evolved ways of it reaching the female part of another plant by using the wind or by 'hitching a lift' on a flying insect. That meeting is called pollination.

Non-flowering plants that make seeds, such as the pine tree (*Pinaccae* sp.) reproduce cones. The cones are unique to each kind of tree and have scales, which when young are closed and show a distinct pattern on the outside of the cone. As they develop, the scales open. Inside are two ovules, which are fertilised by pollen, and then a smooth kind of scale grows over them. This leaves the cone and may be seen as a papery structure with the seed inside. In pines, the young cones are green and small but change as they mature. Pollen is blown across them by the wind and it lands on the open scales. An old cone is dry, brown with the scales open and it falls from the tree (Tunnicliffe and Ueckert, 2011).

Amongst animals which move, there has to be a way for the set of instructions to be carried to the female. Animals that live in water, for example a frog, use the water to help it reproduce. A male frog grips the back of a female and as she lays her eggs he lays his sperm and the eggs are fertilised and can be seen as frogspawn. Without water, those animals that live on land have a different challenge. Scorpions for example make a 'package' and deposit it on the ground, a female will sit on the 'package' and it enters her body. In humans, the male has to use a tube to connect with the female. The half chromosome sets are within a special cell with a tail (this is called a sperm) so it can swim through fluid to reach the female egg. Some mosses, non-flowering plants, have motile sperm which swim to the female part. Spores, equivalent to the seeds of flowering plants, are then produced and released into the air to develop into new plants. Ferns have similar mechanisms. Spores are formed on the rear side of the fern fronds. Ask your children if they have seen these brown shapes on the fronds. They contain the spores which develop into a small, flat plant with male and female plants. The developed egg grows the new fern.

Mating behaviours in some animals can be observed in school. Birds in the immediate environment may display their courting behaviour, for example. Brine shrimps – which can be kept in school (see CLEAPSS, 2005), exhibit particular behaviours with the male swimming underneath the female and fertilisation can then occur. Studying such animals can be useful in personal and social relationship education (Tunnicliffe and Reiss, 1999).

Change is a fundamental part of living things. Plants and animals are dynamic and are constantly changing both form and function. The talking points and activities suggested may assist in developing learners' understanding of the changing nature of the life of plants and animals and, indeed, themselves, as well as the challenge of producing new life in varying habitats. Parents of whatever kind must provide for their offspring until they can fend for themselves and start their own life cycle to produce the next generation. All new life has, in some way, to reproduce itself. That is what life is all about in the most simplest terms.

Conclusion

Living things grow from their smallest beginnings to the adult form which can make more of their kind (reproduce). Children are fascinated by their own growth and development and observe this in other animals and plants. They may be confused and perplexed that young animals and plants do not always resemble the adult parents exactly. Two individuals who often look different from each other are needed to create new ones like themselves. The children gradually learn this basic 'big' idea. They also learn how adults age with time and, eventually, stop living.

References

Birmingham, D. (2018) *Relationships and Sex Education.* Postnote No. 576, June 2018. London: Parliamentary Office of Science and Technology.

Bruner, J.S., Goodnow, J.J. and Austin, G.A. (1956) *A Study of Thinking.* Oxford: John Wiley & Sons.

Cassidy, M. and Tranter, J. (1996) Animals. In Reiss, M. (ed), *Living Biology in Schools.* London: Institute of Biology, pp. 49–66.

CLEAPSS (Consortium of Local Education Authorities for the Provision of Science Services). (2005) Housing and keeping animals, L56, s. 7.5.2. Beetles, pp. 24–25.

Reiss, M. and Tunnicliffe, S.D. (2012) Dioramas as depictions of reality and opportunities for learning in biology. *Curator* 54(4): 447–459.

Tunnicliffe, S.D. (2000) Boys and girls asking questions about pregnancy and birth in primary school. Paper given at the British Educational Research Association Annual Conference, Cardiff University, 7–10 September. Available at: www.leeds.ac.uk/bei/Education-line/browse/all_i tems/112153.html.

Tunnicliffe, S.D. (2010) Another dilemma: birth education or sex education? *Journal of Biological Education,* 44(4): 147–148.

Tunnicliffe, S.D. (2016) Observing mealworms in the primary classroom. *Journal of Emergent Science,* 11: 23–24.

Tunnicliffe, S.D. and Reiss, M.J. (1999) Opportunities for sex education and personal and social education (PSE) through science lessons: the comments of primary pupils when observing meal worms and brine shrimps. *International Journal of Science Education,* 21(9): 1007–1020. DOI: 10.1080/09500699929028.

Tunnicliffe, S.D. and Ueckert, C. (2011) Early biology: the critical years for learning. *Journal of Biological Education,* 45(4): 173–175. DOI: 10.1080/00219266.2010.548873.

Chapter 6

Naming living things

Introduction

Observation in early years children is essential to the development of emergent scientists – it is one of the most important skills to be acquired (Johnston, 2005). Home and direct observation are more important sources of knowledge to children than school. This was the case for both girls and boys (Tunnicliffe and Reiss, 1999, 2000). Working with pre-school children is a balance between children being able to discover for themselves and appropriate adult support (Lloyd et al., 2017), no more so than in exploring the living world.

Some adults consider the terms 'vertebrate' and 'invertebrate', let alone 'chordate', too difficult for children. Is this the reason voiced by adult non-biologists for talking about 'minibeasts', not you may note, 'megabeasts'? There is an erroneous belief in teaching young children that they cannot cope with complex names. I was told by the person who introduced the term 'minibeast' that primary school children found the correct words too difficult. This has not been my experience with children. Children in the English-speaking world seem adept at learning names, for instance such as those of the Pokémon characters or the Latin names of dinosaurs; they enjoy learning names and they remember them (Balmford et al., 2002). I have always found even pre-school children love to use long names and being able to use these marks a breakthrough in the first stages of language acquisition.

There is an apparent conflict of interest for children learning to name living things, between the 'experts' scientific name, the everyday name used in general, and the children's first and personal names they give things as they start to recognise differences between plants and animals. Whilst specialised taxonomic knowledge is not necessary for adults with these emergent biologists, a basic understanding of taxonomic hierarchies of popular plants and animals is needed.

> The experiences which children have of adults using language with them must play an important part in influencing the kind of interpretation that children will make of their everyday experiences. If for example, the adult is talking about particular detail in the environment, the structure of plants, the shape and colour of the rainbow, the reflections in puddles, then the child's attention is being drawn to objects that he might not have noticed had no one spoken to him about them, or, if he had, might have remained at a level of interpretation that did not require conscious awareness of detail ...
>
> (Tough, 1977, p. 35)

How children learn the names of plants and animals

Adults use language to direct children and to manage them. For example, in a museum the parent or teacher may be seen instructing children to look at this or that and asking questions, or controlling the length of time the children are looking at things. Children need time to 'stand and stare' at things. When able to observe things first hand, emergent biologists begin to learn more and more about organisms (Tunnicliffe, 2011, 2016). Adults play a vital role in this process. Choosing names and categories of plants and animals which they see in their environment to inform the children is important. But some everyday names can be misleading, such as calling whales 'fish' or birds 'not animals'. I found young children in England thought the word 'grass' was synonymous with lawn and that 'plant' was the word for the action of planting a flower in a plant pot.

Very young children, for example my youngest son, inexperienced in seeing a variety of mammals, named any animal that resembled a dog (i.e. had hair and four legs and that moved) as a dog. Although this is a personal observation on him, I have also found this to be the case with many other very young children. Trowbridge and Mintzes (1985) considered that whatever the biological name children ultimately arrive at for an animal, the decision for a name is based on relative size or perceived importance of its body parts, their everyday knowledge of animals and inherent categorisation tendencies (Tversky, 1989), and not on zoological knowledge. The same applies to plants.

Markman (1989, p. 16) wrote that if a concept is to be learnt and understood it develops first from what children already know and then to acquire the new concept, the child needs to have analytic abilities and break down the object/event into its component properties. Children should say what they think something is, and why they think this, and then see if this matches what scientists think. One 8 year old, when taken to a natural history museum with taxidermically preserved animals was curious. The specimens looked like animals but they didn't move. So he then asked his mother if they were statues. Children match organisms in the living world with specimens for which they already know a name using the appearance of an animal or plant to decide what kind it is. By 9 years of age many are able to recognise which major category it belongs and also explain the characteristics with others, thus children start using exemplars when naming.

In order to acquire both an everyday and scientific understanding of an animal or plant, and its appropriate taxonomic position, children must perceive the appropriate characteristics of the organism, for the ability to categorise using either everyday or biological taxonomy is based on recognising a set of attributes, which have to be learnt. Sometimes adults with children may impose a taxonomy of their own or the simple science one. It is important to listen to the names the children may use and talk about them before introducing more biological terms. Such instances of alternative names to the common everyday ones or scientific ones provide an opportunity to restructure or extend the child's existing concepts. A general rule that many children learn early on is that if an organism is green and doesn't move around from place to place it is a plant, but if it is not green and moves around it is an animal. Adults, as well as children, also use animal behaviour and habitats in allocating an organism, plant or animal to a category. Dolphins, which swim, usually in seas, and have a streamlined fish-like shape, are frequently grouped with fish. Cacti, when seen in an exhibit, usually elicit remarks like, 'This must be a desert because there are cacti!'.

Talk science: what animal, plant or neither?

When you are outdoors there are probably some plants and a few animals, e.g. cats, dogs and birds. There are also likely to be non-living things such as cars or street 'furniture', like post boxes, lights, waste bins and seats.

Point out something and ask: what do you think this is? Is it a plant or an animal? Why do you think that? What does it have that is like something else you know?

 Activity: grouping

With very young children choose some objects they like: toys of different colours and perhaps soft toy animals. Ask them to sort them into groups with you. What do they name the groups? Why? Do they put all the red objects together, or the blue ones? Do they place large and small ones separately? Can they make subgroups within each group, for example, big red things and small red things?

 Activity: plant bits!

Try a similar activity with plant materials, perhaps leaves of differing colours and shapes such as holly, pine, willow and ginkgo, rose petals, grass. Watch and listen how they group them. Provide stems with leaves and no flowers as well as some stems with leaves and flowers, and, if you can, a flower on a stem and no leaves so the child can divide the collection into leaves, leaves and flowers, and flowers only.

A child has to learn the names of phenomena to be able to communicate and retain this knowledge into adulthood, gradually expanding it. Names of things are the first words to be learnt from an ever-growing circle of others with whom s/he communicates. Bruner, Goodnow and Austin (1956, p. 8) maintain that concepts are acquired first and are built up from perceptions of the learner. In the category of living things they learn to tell the difference between members, basically plants and animals, then between smaller groups, such as mammals and birds, flowering plants and non-flowering plants and the living and dead. The 'artificial' groupings of botany, for example, are terms such as fruits, vegetables and weeds amongst plants, which children hear adults frequently use. These are not scientific groupings but utilitarian ones of everyday.

Activity: grouping foods from plants

Try the grouping activity with the plant parts which we eat: stems, roots, fruits, leaves and flowers, such as celery, carrots, bananas, apples, tomatoes, potatoes, cauliflower and lettuce. Often children begin grouping by colour and size, such as 'red' or 'big', and not a taxonomic hierarchy – an easier task because the plants are effectively being allocated to a collection or theme that suits the child.

According to Piaget and Inhelder (1969, p. 101), children begin classifying objects by arranging them according to their increasing size. For example, they recognise this is a tree and belongs to a wood, but that a wood is not a tree. Once they can recognise a few kinds of trees they can say a tree belongs in a wood. The tendency of young children to group objects by size is characteristic of the earliest stages in classification (Inhelder and Piaget, 1964, p. 7). A mother or other adult points in the zoo or in a book to a lion she means for the child to learn the word 'lion' to be associated with the whole body. Often for example an adult will teach the child the word 'mane' and will point out that part of the lion's body.

We as adults have this layered alternate terminology with body parts too when we talk with children. The lower front of the human body is the abdomen, often referred to in popular conversations as the stomach or tummy. In my experience, most adults, when talking with children, call the abdomen the 'tummy'. We select the name to describe that to which we are referring in conversation to fit the people with whom we are talking. We do this without thinking, although research shows that adults tend to use the 'basic' term, that is the one most often used in everyday dialogue, when we talk with children.

However, young children can and do learn to group animals within a taxonomy. They learn that an animal belongs with others that look similar and can be grouped together sharing some non-special features into larger and larger inclusive categories. For example, pet cat – all cats – mammal – animal. The reasoning for a simple hierarchy is the fact that the animals have four legs, so they are boned animals, vertebrates, but they have fur too and a tail so must be a mammal, and then they belong to the vertebrate group with four limbs, a head and a tail. They all have four limbs but they are not always all legs. If it has two legs, two wings and feathers it must be a bird, but that also belongs to the big vertebrate group along with mammals, fish, reptiles and amphibians. Children seem to find this basic categorising easier for animals than plants. Often children work out the group to which something belongs by noticing what the plant or animal has.

Beginning to name living things

Children make up their own classifications from what they observe. Even before they talk they do this and once they can start naming out loud it provides an opportunity for a dialogue with someone else. Very often, even when a toddler is not speaking yet, adults notice what they are looking at and will tell them the name. This is a labelling process, a very human need. Dialogues are initiated by the adult's words, repeated by the child and then the dialogue closed by the adult. This is known as a triadic dialogue, of three parts, with two speakers – an adult who starts and closes the dialogue with a respondent in the middle (Lemke, 1990, p. 11). Such form of talk is heard often in lessons and when other people are testing someone. For example, a 'teacher' type of dialogue used by adults to children:

Parent to child (at a farm): What is that?
Child: A cow.
Parent: No, it is a bull.

An extended triadic teaching dialogue may be seen in the following example, when a school group was looking at penguins:

Teacher: What colour are they?
Girl 1: Black and white.
Teacher: What are they covered by?
Girl 1: Feathers.
Girl 2: I can't see.

An inverse triadic dialogue, 'Wavy Bits' is as follows. I heard this dialogue in an aquarium with an early years child (boy):

Boy: What are those things with wavy bits?
Adult: They are sea anemones.
Boy: Sea anemones, Sea anemones.

Observing anemones in a tank, another boy initiated the following exchange:

Boy: Are those tomato fish?
Adult: No, sea anemones.
Boy: They look like tomato fish to me.

Child to child, often called peer talk, is characterised by a triadic dialogue and occurs frequently when a few children look together at plants and animals.

They have the following structure with one child being in the role of initiator and another child as respondent.

Girl 1: Look at that fish, it's got writing on its side.
Girl 2: Which one?
Girl 1: That big one there.

Adults use some dialogues as a way of finding out (summative assessment) the child's understanding. Hence, the following exchange in a reptile house at a zoo, at an exhibit containing lizards (reptiles) with primary school children aged 8 to 9:

Adult: What is his skin made of?
Boy: Scales.

This dialogue is another form of assessment. The receiver, the child, acknowledged the question, which s/he answered with a first-hand observation.

Adult: Did you see the snake?
Boy: They are slithery, snakes.

The child's talk is initiated and closed by the child in reverse of the adult 'teacher'; conversations when the child begins and closes the short dialogue (Patrick and Tunnicliffe, 2011, p. 107). This is straightforward instructional dialogue.

Learning to name

My work with families or school groups in biological collections, plant and animal, are concerned with allocating names to individual animals or plant specimens. However, Donaldson (1978, p. 92) points out that a request from a young child for the name of an object, or for an explanation, is part of a child's acquisition of the characteristics of the object, not necessarily an overt need for categorisation. Once any of us know a name of something it is easier to refer to it to others. It is an understood shorthand. A child's recognition of animals which he identified as birds on a visit to a zoo is an example of this phenomenon. It is the start of learning biological categorisation.

 Talk science: what's your name?

When you see a plant ask, 'Do you know the name of that plant?' You are identifying its largest membership category! 'Does it remind you of another plant you know?' 'What is it that you think is like the other plant?'

Children learn to notice the features of plants and animals, and other things in their lives, from observing the organism as a whole, and this is vital in being able to decide what it is. Tversky (1989) showed that children are more likely to group objects taxonomically when they share parts they can see than when they do not. Perceptually obvious, or salient parts, such as those of differing shape or large size, were detected faster by young children. Indeed, children do notice and use the shape and size of objects, along with any prominent features in their categorisation and recognition of things, including of animals and plants. For example, for an animal, a large tail, the trunk of an elephant or wing of a bird may be used, while for a plant they may use the very spiky-edged leaves of a holly or the needle shaped leaves of the conifer. In the beginning of learning, children recognise a few individuals with a type or group name, such as not 'snake' but 'python', not 'fish' but 'shark'. The ability to classify objects in a hierarchy requires a grasp of class inclusion, that is a recognition of what

92 Naming living things

features something has to have that other things in the group also have – an ability that requires abstract thought. Such an ability plays a crucial role in a child's further development of concepts and classification. Keil (1979) researched the development of understanding categories and found that 5-year-old children, and some younger, have the potential to organise categories hierarchically, from many smaller ones to a bigger category and then to even bigger categories still. He also found, however, that the hierarchical tree of the children was small. They could place an organism into an animal or plant group and then put animals in to a smaller group, for example mammal, when they saw a dog. Adults should start using animals with which the children are familiar with and thus build upon their understanding when helping them learn to group with reasons.

During a visit with his family to an aquarium, an early-years-aged boy said that an animal he recognised could be called both a fish and a shark. When he asked what another animal was he claimed fish was only the other name for a shark. His elder brother held this dialogue at the same exhibit:

Michael: Yes, these are sharks, look!
Aunt: How can you tell?
Michael: Because they are dead long and have tails like that. That's not a shark though (bat fish). I expect that's its food.
Aunt: Why is that not a shark?
Michael: That's their food probably.
Aunt: But how do you know it's not a shark?
Michael: Because it's flat.

The greater the variety of animal and plant forms that children see and the more they practise grouping them according to different criterial attributes, such as visual body features and non-visual structures including habitats or behaviours, the easier they will find it to learn the basic names for the animals and begin to recognise the criterial attributes of what scientists call something to the everyday name we all use. The role of the school, home and plant and animal collections is to widen children's visual perceptions of the variety of animals and plants and begin to teach the ways in which these can be both named and grouped, leading the children eventually into biological taxonomy. Enabling these observations of plants and animals is very much an instinctive activity which families do too. It is part of their learning journey together.

Issues in learning to name

Keil (1979) considers that 'animal' is one of a human being's fundamental ontological concepts. Children learn to recognise that certain 'things' are alive before they can justify the categorisation of the item (Looft, 1971).

Using a word does not mean the user shares the same understanding of the concept incorporated in the language as the listener (Donaldson, 1978, p. 92). To acquire both everyday and scientific understanding of an organism and its appropriate taxonomic position for naming, children must perceive the appropriate characteristics of the animal. Being able to name and categorise using either everyday or biological taxonomy is based on recognising a set of attributes, largely visual, which must be learnt. People look at living things and name them all the time and children overhear. However, overhearing out of context can cause difficulties and affect the ability of others in the group, who had not previously known a name, being influenced by one member. The name may be incorrect.

If the learner does not know the identity of something they see they will name it as if it were the plant or animal of which it reminds them. A 2-year-old boy at a nursery group was shown some mealworms, the larvae of a flour beetle (*Tenebrio sp.*), and immediately announced they, '… were worms'. They do have a segmented body, but the resemblance ends there!

Other children meeting mealworms (see Chapter 3) refer to mealworms as 'maggots', if they have ever seen blowfly larvae (commonly called maggots) on meat left out and on which flies have landed, or if they know about fishing where maggots are used as bait.

Gradual learning of identity, one feature at a time

Embedded knowledge, as presented in a hierarchical naming system, is not present in the 'ad hoc' themes or collections (Markman, 1989, pp. 78–84), such as calling some boneless animals, like ants, spiders and beetles, 'creepy crawlies', which may be preferred by the children or the institution, but the use of which does not assist in children's learning of zoological nomenclature and taxonomy. It is similar to referring to a plant growing where you do not want it to as a 'weed'. Themes or collections are easier to use than hierarchies because they employ only one dimension or attribute. The name that we give to an organism when we talk about it is a shorthand code. The 'code' contains much more information you can work out. It is a summary, if it is understood – a shorthand way of referring to that living thing and what it is. Table 6.1 may be used as a guide to an animal you know and its name so you can find a related animal. Answer the questions for an animal you know. You have to look closely at your animal.

 Talk science: which animal group am I?

Choose a familiar animal that a child knows, e.g. a cat. Ask them what its name is. They may give its group name, e.g. a cat, or they may give its own name, e.g. Tiggy. Which name do they give? Is it the name, e.g. Tiggy, which tells you it is a pet? If they say cat, ask what that tells you about the animal. Ask what group of animal it belongs to. What does the name 'cat' mean? What else can it tell you? (It shares features with other cats.) All cats also share features with other animals. What are they? (Mammals with four legs and fur.)

 Activity: which plant?

Try the same pattern of dialogue with a plant you all know. *Mystery*: what am I? Where do I belong? Perhaps a 'What's my shorthand sheet' would help?

94 Naming living things

Table 6.1 What's my name?

Everyday name. All about our ...

What kind of animal? What are the special features?

What do all members of that group have in common?

What are they all called?

What bigger group do they all belong to, e.g. cats were all carnivores (carnivores are mammals)?

Is there another group for these animals with a name of the category that tells you more (mammals are vertebrates)?

Does this big group belong to another bigger group?

> (Technically all boned animals, vertebrates, are chordates because they all have a post-anal tail that can be seen. Other features are internal and the important one is a notochord, which develops in boned animals into the spinal cord inside the vertebral column.)

Does this big group belong to another bigger group?

Animals

People may not always look for criteria when they are categorising. They may adopt a non-analytic approach using overall similarities of the unknown object to known examples, thus establishing categories according to resemblance with the exemplar (Markman, 1989, p. 63). Using overall similarity would prevent children from 'prematurely settling on dimensions that might turn out to be wrong'. A 7-year-old boy, when visiting a zoo, categorised the Bateleur Eagle as 'bird' but did not categorise it any further, presumably because the specimen did not match any specific bird exemplar that he held. However, when he saw the penguins he was able to identify them as penguins at once – members of a smaller category of bird and sharing features of birds, like feathers and a beak, but also having unique penguin features like walking upright, swimming and having very reduced wings. Giving something a name is of paramount importance for children (Tunnicliffe, 1996).

Using the most obvious features – of plants and animals

As discussed earlier, young children and adults will both notice and name the most striking features of organisms and categorise or name them from those. This means when children look at animals and try to name them they describe noticeable features, such as prominent parts of the body which stick out – horns, tails, legs, wings, colours and shapes. They also notice obvious behaviours, like flying, swimming, fighting, eating or running (Tunnicliffe, 1996; Reiss and Tunnicliffe, 2000). They notice unusual aspects too of plants, particular colour and smell as well as having an urge to touch particular leaves and petals.

Categories in general have 'best examples', or prototypes. Categorisation is 'essentially a matter of both human experience and imagination'. According to Lakoff (1987, p. 8), 5 year olds used appearance to put what they are looking at in a category. However, according to Keil (reported by Carey, 1985, p. 178ff), 9 year olds understand that a name tells you what natural group the organism belongs to because the organism shares observable features with other organisms in the same group. A toddler remarked on seeing a caterpillar, 'Little worm! A little worm, there!'.

Smell is important to young children when looking at plants, particularly herbaceous flowering ones. A 6-year-old boy remarked, 'Let's see what it smells like! Ugh! It smells like poo', yet the flower was actually a rose! Lavender and rose plants have distinct identifiable smells or perfumes. If children are allowed to touch the leaves and crush them, those for example of mint or rosemary, they enjoy doing that. They also enjoy stroking leaves with hairs on, which feel furry. To a much lesser extent in my experience, children use smell and touch in naming animals, but some odours do indicate the presence of some animals, such as house mice or dead animals.

Talk science: observing plants around us

What plants do you know? What kinds of plants are they? What plants can we see out of our kitchen, living room or bedroom window? Do they live in the ground or somewhere else?

Show me those with thick woody stems or trunks. What do you call them? How do you know what they are? Which plants grow very close to the ground? What are the tallest plants we can see? Where do they grow?

Activity: your name for plants

Which words do you, as a grown up, use for biological organisms that you see? Make a list of those names which you use for organisms when you talk with other adults and the names you give to the same organisms when talking to children of differing ages. Point out plants you and the children can both see (inside and out!). Ask them what they call them and why.

Hearing and grouping

Using a word does not mean the user shares the same understanding of the concept incorporated in the language as the listener (Inhelder and Piaget, 1964, p. 7; Donaldson, 1978, p. 92). In order to acquire both everyday and scientific understanding of an animal and its appropriate taxonomic position, children must perceive the appropriate characteristics of the animal, for the ability to categorise using either everyday or biological taxonomy is based on recognising a set of attributes, which have to be learnt. Thus, the experiences for visitors within an animal or plant collection which the organisers, i.e. the adult in charge, may impose a taxonomy on the names the child is using before the child is ready to learn that too. Doing this may cause some difficulty for children but it can also provide an opportunity to restructure or extend concepts, which includes names the child has not met before. Different languages have more distinct words for animals and the different kinds, whereas in English 'animal' is also used in everyday talk to mean mammal. Villabi and Lucas (1991) showed that the confusion between 'everyday' and 'scientific' senses of the term 'animal' did not occur amongst Catalan or Castilian speakers, and their finding raises the issue of applicability of research findings that are concerned with language from one linguistic group to another. Therefore, if adults and children do not share the same meaning, misunderstandings can arise.

What is a plant? Plants everyday and plant blindness

Children are not informed as often about plants as they are about animals (Lindemann-Matthies, 2005). People often ignore plants because they are still, whereas they notice a moving animal. This phenomenon is known as 'plant blindness' (Wandersee and Schussler, 1999). Gradually, children do name and group both. Donaldson (1978, p. 92) points out that when a child requests a name or explanation of something, it is part of a child's process of acquiring its dimensions – the unique defining essence of something. An 8-year-old visiting a zoo with her family identified a flamingo as such, but other birds in the same enclosure she said were 'birds' (they were pelicans), both animals fitted her understanding of the dimensions of bird and such is the precursor, the initial stage needed before they can categorise. Similarly, a 5-year-old girl in a garden standing by a flowerbed remarked, 'A flower, it's got a flower!'

Children soon learn which animals and plants belong together, or category inclusion, in which things are all members of the same group or category. For example, they can distinguish between different kinds of categories of flowers, or learn that caterpillar and butterfly, tadpole and frog, are different forms of the same thing and are just at different stages of life. They follow the everyday classification they hear too, such as fruits and vegetables, weeds and plants and trees. Category definition tends to be the superordinate all-inclusive categories such as fish, birds, and the use of the word 'animal' meaning mammals. If, for instance, they see pigeons, they know they are birds, but also called 'pigeon', so the basis of their category membership is being formed.

The same occurs amongst children, and indeed many adults, when using the term 'plants' to mean plants with flowers. They call anything above the height of many branched and bushy plants, 'bushes', and plants, which grow upwards with a thick stem, or trunk, 'trees'. Some plants known as trees are, in biological terms, not trees, an example being a palm tree –

it is not woody inside nor does it have branches, all its leaves are at the top of the stem. It is an herbaceous plant. Technically, a tree is a woody plant (with a definite hard outside layer, is a perennial, grows for many years and usually has a single upright stalk or stem, known as a trunk, which can grow very high compared with non trees). Trees have side branches too, coming off the bare lower stem, some way from the ground.

Children will notice the unusual in a plant just as they do when looking at animals. Whilst in a horticultural garden on a school visit, a child remarked at a clump of plants belonging to the *Gunnera* species (giant rhubarb), which have large prickly stems and enormous, almost umbrella-like leaves, 'Wow! Look at those leaves. I have never seen a plant with such big leaves!'. Carnivorous plants also intrigue children during visits to botanical gardens. They asked what would happen if they inserted their finger in a Venus Fly trap leaf.

Thus, 'plant' is a term restricted in the everyday understanding of many people in the developed world to refer to the small herbaceous angiosperms also referred to as flowers.

 Talk science: plants we see everyday

Talk about which plants you see regularly, in the street, at the shops, in books.

 Activity: plant i-spy

Play i-spy when in a garden with different kinds of plants. Modify the rules as appropriate, for example allow them to say 'Cold! Getting warm!' in response to your answer. You must both be able to see the plant if the child is young. Choose obvious plants such as a brightly coloured flowering plant, a tree standing by itself, grass plants forming a lawn.
Say:

'Choose a plant you know.'
'Don't tell me I have to guess and you have to answer only yes or no.'
'Is it a tall plant or a short plant?'
'Has it a stem?'
'Has it several stems growing up and outwards?'
'Has it or had it leaves?'
'Are the leaves needle-like or flat and all the same shape?'
'Are the leaves on all year, because it is an evergreen?'
'Has it flowers?'
'Does it grow in a flower bed or a plant pot?'

Activity: rhymes

Can you make up a rhyme using the names of some plants or animals? Suggest some names that you know you have looked at or talked about with the child.

Activity: word search

Make up a word search which has four names in it and challenge the child to find the names. Choose names that they have talked about and seen. Do a word search for plants, one for animals, one for plants and animals, for example. Start simply, for example using the words plant, tree, flower and seed, and insert your chosen terms on a grid drawn on squared paper, for example a grid six squares by six squares. Write in your words then fill in the blank squares with random letters.

Activity: what's my name challenge

Show a plant of your choosing and ask, 'What am I?'. Let the child say what they think. You can ask them to tell you what they know and of what other plant the chosen plant reminds them of. Have they seen a plant like this one anywhere else? Try to choose a few plants that you are sure that they know!

Knowing where things live but not their name!

Children observe living things long before they know their names. Children know that certain animals live on the ground but others live in water and yet others in the air.

When children of 5, 8, 10, and 14 years old were shown six species of live plants (and a fungus, an edible mushroom bought from a shop to be accurate) they all recognised the plants and used anatomical features when naming them and explaining why they are what they are. Recognition, but no name was quite common amongst children (Tunnicliffe and Reiss, 2000). Some pupils used habitat features where the plants were likely to be found, such as mosses in a damp place, perhaps at the bottom of a shaded wall, but had no name for the plant or its group.

Naming living things 99

 Activity: guess my name

Devise, with or for learners, a mystery. The child chooses a plant or an animal of which they know. Then the devisor must tell the person to work out the name of the organism, giving only one fact about the organism, such as 'I have fur'. You reply with a guess. If it is incorrect they have to tell you another statement and you answer with another guess before they give you a further clue statement, such as 'I live in houses, if I can'.

 Activity: tell me!

'What does your plant look like?'
'Do you think it will be there to see tomorrow?'
'Will it look the same or different'?
'Next week? This time next year? Why? How?'
'Will it always look the same or do you think it will change?'
'If so, what do you think will look the same or different?'
'Why do you think that? What do you remember?'
'Will it always have that name?'
'Will there always be flowers or do they change into something else with another name?'

 Activity: plant watch!

Show the child some plants they have seen and of which they may know the name of. I suggest a tree, an herbaceous plant and a flowering houseplant. Can the child name them so they know which is which? Take a photograph of the chosen plants. Take another photograph of the plants next week. Compare the photographs; are they similar or has the plant changed?

Real? Dead? Alive?

Is it real? This is a frequent question from young children, and some adults, particularly at animals on exhibit or an organism seen in the field that is inanimate.

Children have problems in their early years distinguishing between living things and non-living because they associate moving with being alive, hence clouds and fire are moving, thus must be alive. They will be learning extensively, long before the start of formal teaching. Many biological organisms appear inanimate much of the time. I have heard young children and, in fact adults, looking at alligators in zoos announcing that the animal is a model or dead, because it is not moving. Therefore, telling young children that plants are alive does not fit with their idea or understanding of 'aliveness'. Children between the ages of 4 and 6 begin, for the first time, to use the concept of 'life' and being 'alive' to predict and explain biological phenomena, and it is at this age that a biological construction of their knowledge about life begins. However, dead and dying, hence no longer being alive and not coming back to life, is a more difficult concept and is not thought to begin to be understood until children are at least 6 or 7 years of age. Skeletons do cause misunderstandings because of the way they are portrayed in museums, articulated in the shape of the animal or in books or animation cartoons as running around without flesh or a body covering. Children have to learn that skeletons, without the ligaments holding bones together would just be heaps of all the bones.

The question 'Is it the real thing?' is an important consideration when listening and seeking to understand children's responses and the sense they make. There have been few studies comparing children's responses to undoubtedly 'authentic' live animals or plants in zoos or various gardens or outdoors, with responses to preserved animals and models in museums. These distinctions, and children's understanding of the categories of living things, are vital if children are to learn about the living world and the place of living things in various habitats.

It is important to remember that children will resort to interpretations of what they see and base it on fantasy when they have no concrete knowledge upon which to call. 'Dead' and the use of the word 'real' are important terms for children. They equate stillness to being 'dead' or being a model, and use the word 'real' to apply to living organisms in contrast to those which are deemed 'dead'. Authenticity and realness are important issues for children looking at organisms.

 Talk science: alive?

As you walk around in a room or outside, ask children: 'Is this alive?' 'How do you know?' Talk about what they think.

 Activity: alive?

Show a collection of familiar items – a model farm animal, a soft toy animal, a pebble, some very small pebbles, dry seeds (like nasturtium, dried peas or similar). Ask them if each item is alive. How do they know?

Children have a criteria by which they deem an animal to be judged to be alive and known as an animal. Various research studies reveal that autonomous movement by the object is the most often used criterion for judging whether something is alive, although the making of sound by an animal is also very important to certain children. Plants, however, are different. Although a living plant is green, dried or dead plants are brown, as in

Naming living things 101

dead leaves or herbaceous plants. Dead leaves, being dry and crackly, make a noise when you walk through them on the ground in autumn. Dryness as well as 'floppy' herbaceous plants are the main criteria that young children use.

Seeds, alive or not?

Seeds intrigue children – are they alive or not? Seeds can enter a state of suspended animation in which they can exist for hundreds of years before then growing. The Millennium Seedbank at Wakehurst Place, part of Kew Gardens, aims to preserve the world's plants. They aim, by gradually banking seeds from wild plants around the world, to retain diversity. They have 15 percent of seeds so far. Bell (1981) found that by the age of 11, school children in New Zealand did not consider seeds to be plants until they had grown, indeed the dormant state of seeds leads many children to consider them not to be alive. Jewell (2002), in a study with primary children from reception (4–5 year olds) to the primary school leaving age (11–12 years), showed them some seeds from different sources – some from fruits like apple and orange seeds, pine cones with seeds on seed leaves, some nuts, some straight from a seed packet (Nasturtium and Lobelia), and some non-seeds like potatoes, onions, an egg and a packet of sweets. The logic being that an egg has a seed-like shape and does contain an embryo (potentially!). Seeds were shown in their context. For example, the apple seeds are in in the middle of an apple so were shown in a cut in half apple alongside a whole apple. Peas were in a whole pod as well as shown in one opened. Packet seeds were shown in the open packet. Children recognised apple and orange seeds, familiar with food, but children had planted them to grow. Children with whom I have worked with also thought seeds were not alive because they showed no sign of growth but thought seeds could 'become alive' if planted.

 Talk science: getting to know a seed

'What is a seed'? 'Where do you find seeds?' 'How can you tell something is a seed?' 'Do seeds always stay seeds?' 'What are seeds for?'

 Activity: where do seeds come from?

Collect some fruits and seeds and try to find the seeds inside the fruit with your child.
Collect two apples (one whole and one cut in half), and two oranges, lemons or grapefruits (one peeled with segments showing the seeds and one whole), a small potato, a small onion, a nut, some seeds from a commercial packet and two mangetout pods (fruits) (one open to show the seeds, beans and pod).

If you are doing this out of season, show the seeds dry and use photographs of the pods (which are really fruits with seeds in them). Ask the children what they are. If they do not know, point out a seed and ask what it is for.

Conclusion

Children need to hear the language and names that other adults call living things – plants, animals and their habitats, and behaviours. Very young children, emergent biologists, if they have not heard the name of something may make up one from their existing repertoire, and this may be descriptive of the things appearance, of what they think the organisms do or of their habitat. There is a category in everyday parlance to which most people allocate an organism if they recognise some characteristic of a group but not anymore specific defining criteria. Examples are 'bird' or a more specific species name such as robin or swan. Small herbaceous flowering plants which are seen most often by many young children, are frequently allocated to the group 'plant' (a herbaceous plant with a flower) or a 'tree' (a woody, seed-bearing plant). Without names for things, humans are at a loss, being unable to categorise their world and share this information. Seeing organisms, whether it be in books, other media or in real life, and hearing their names is an important aspect of helping children learn names, and a very necessary condition for subsequent learning and discussion.

References

Balmford, A., Clegg, L., Coulson, T. and Taylor, J. (2002) Why conservationists should heed Pokémon. *Science*, 295(5564): 2367.

Bell, B. (formerly, Stead, B.) (1980) Plants. LISP Working Paper 24, *Science Education Research*, University of Waikato, Hamilton, New Zealand.

Bell, B. (1981) When is an animal not an animal? *Journal of Biological Education*, 15: 202–218.

Bruner, J.S., Goodnow, J.J. and Austin, G.A. (1956) *A Study of Thinking*. New York: Transaction Publishers.

Carey, S. (1985) *Cognitive Change in Children*. Cambridge, MA: The MIT Press.

Donaldson, M. (1978) *Children's Minds*. London: Fontana.

Inhelder, B. and Piaget, J. (1964) *The Early Growth of Logic in the Child: Classification and Seriation.* London: Routledge & Kegan Paul.

Jewell, N.M. (2002) Examining children's models of seed. *Journal of Biological Education*, 33(3): 116–122. DOI: 10.1080/00219266.2002.9655816.

Johnston, J. (2005) *Early Explorations in Science*. Maidenhead, UK: Open University Press, p. 33.

Keil, F. (1979) *Semantic and Conceptual Development: An Ontological Perspective*. Cambridge, MA: Harvard University Press.

Lakoff, G. (1987) *Women, Fire, and Dangerous Things: What Categories Reveal About the Mind.* London: University of Chicago Press, p. 8. ISBN: 0226468038.

Lemke, J. (1990) *Talking Science: Language, Learning and Values*. Norwood, NJ: Ablex Publishing Corporation.

Lindemann-Matthies, P. (2005) 'Loveable' mammals and 'lifeless' plants: how children's interest in common local organisms can be enhanced through observation of nature. *International Journal of Science Education*, 27(6): 655–677.

Lloyd, E., Edmonds, C., Downs, C., Crutchley, R. and Paffard, F. (2017) Talking science to very young children: a study involving parents and practitioners within an early childhood centre. *Early Child Development and Care*, 197(2): 224–260.

Looft, R.C. (1971) Children's judgement of age. *Child Development*, 42: 1282–1284.

Markman, E. (1989) *Categorization and Naming in Children: Problems of Induction*. Cambridge, MA: The MIT Press.

Patrick, P. and Tunnicliffe, S.D. (2011) What plants and animals do early childhood and primary students name? Where do they see them? *Journal of Science Education and Technology*, 20(5): 630–642.

Piaget, J. and Inhelder, B. (1969) *The Psychology of the Child*. London: Routledge & Kegan Paul.

Reiss, M. and Tunnicliffe, S.D. (2000) What sense do children make of three-dimensional, life-sized representations of animals? *School Science and Mathematics*, 100(3): 128–138.

Tough, J. (1977) *The Development of Meaning: A Study of Children's Use of Language*. Routledge Library Editions. Abingdon, UK: Routledge.

Trowbridge, J.E. and Mintzes, J.J. (1985) Students alternative conceptions of animals and animal classification. *School Science and Mathematics*, 85(4): 304–316.

Tunnicliffe, S.D. (1996) A comparison of conversations of primary school groups at animated, preserved, and live animal specimens. *Journal of Biological Education*, 30(3): 195–206. DOI: 10.1080/00219266.1996.9655503.

Tunnicliffe, S.D. (2011) Young children as emergent biologists: brine shrimps in the classroom. *Journal of Emergent Science*, 1(2): 25–32.

Tunnicliffe, S.D. (2016) Observing mealworms in the primary classroom. *Journal of Emergent Science*, 11: 23–33.

Tunnicliffe, S.D. and Reiss, M.J. (1999) Building a model of the environment: how do children see animals? *Journal of Biological Education*, 33(3): 142–148. DOI: 10.1080/00219266.1999.9655654.

Tunnicliffe, S.D. and Reiss, M.J. (2000) Building a model of the environment: how do children see plants? *Journal of Biological Education*, 34(4): 172–177.

Tversky, B. (1989) Parts, partonomies and taxonomies. *Developmental Psychology*, 25(6): 983–995.

Villabi, R.M. and Lucas, A.M. (1991) When is an animal not an animal? When it speaks English! *Journal of Biological Education*, 3: 184–186.

Wandersee, J.H. and Schussler, E. (1999) Preventing plant blindness. *The American Biology Teacher*, 61(2) (Feb.): 82–86.

Chapter 7

Earth science
Rocks, soil, weather and habitats

Introduction

The living world is dependent on our planet for its very existence. The Earth, our planet, creates the habitats and the climate in which living organisms exist. The living world uses the laws of physics, e.g. the ability of animals to move from place to place in search of food and to avoid danger. Plants also use laws of physics, e.g. to stay upright in the soil and use light energy to make their 'food'. Thus, understanding the living world means that children should understand these aspects too.

The Earth is a dynamic entity and we humans depend on it, as do all other living things. Earth science studies are central to our understanding of the living world. Without our planet, the Earth, living things and their habitats, including the climate, would not exist (Balmer, 2018). People recognise the importance of looking after our Earth, for all living things depend on it for their very existence. We need a 'sustainable, ecological and living reality' (Arthus-Bertrand, 2008). It is important that young children develop this understanding of their environment and how it works. We need to know our particular place. An understanding of the environment, our place, is crucial in understanding humans as well as the planetary effects that have an impact on the environment, especially if we are to support the continued existence of all life.

The culture in which they lived as children affects adults' ideas according to Unsworth et al. (2012). Medin et al. (2010), however, found that there were no cultural differences in ecological reasoning and psychological closeness to nature between Menominee Native Americans and rural European American adults. They conducted structured interviews with children in which each child viewed several pairs of plant pictures. Their research showed that Native American children (the Menominee), mentioned ecological relations and spiritual links to nature more than European American children. These Native American children (5–7 years of age) made more observations of animals and both mentioned ecological links and mimicked them more than the European American children of the same age. Both sets of children responded to questions about classification and body structure similarly. Tunnicliffe and Reiss (2000), investigating how children built their model of the environment, focusing on animals, found only older children sometimes referred to habitats in their conversations to the researchers about the specimens. These children used morphological features when naming and looked for a 'nearest fit' model when the animal was unfamiliar to them. Leach et al. (1996), in a series of three linked studies in England, studied selected ecological understandings of English school children aged 5–16. The first study explained the methodology of the research. In the second, the researchers looked at the cycling of matter between organisms and their abiotic environment whilst the third study investigated the understanding of interdependency of organisms in ecosystems (Leach et al., 1996).

Our living world

Our living world is often referred to as the 'Blue' planet because of its colour when seen from space, also shows the effect of one species changing not only the physical surface of the Earth, but its biological component, the plants and many other aspects. The rate at which members of one species, the human race, has driven down numbers of other species and caused them to become extinct, such as the classic example of the dodo in Mauritius or the passenger pigeon in the USA, is incredible.

Talk science: where do animals live?

Do you know where different kinds of animals live near you? Where do fish live? Can all fish live in both the sea and fresh water? Where do birds live? Where have you seen birds yourself?

Our living world is dependent on the Earth. Recognising Earth science features that have formed our environment is part of learning biology. Without the Earth, its rocks and its effect on the atmosphere around it we would not have a living world. Earth science is central to the existence of our living world, the landscapes and habitats therein: this is shown in Figure 7.1.

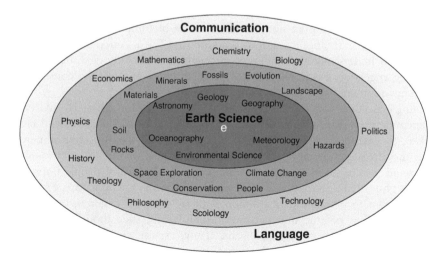

Figure 7.1 The central place of Earth science in our living world
Reproduced courtesy of D. Balmer (2007)

Children learn to recognise differing types of landscapes and the plants and animals that live there. They learn that snow on the ground indicates a certain type of climate and when it is permanent a certain kind of animal adapts to the Earth's covering where they live. Philips (1991) wrote that little work has been done on children's understanding of Earth science. Although in the intervening years since then a few more studies have emerged, it still remains, at least in England, a less studied area. Recognising Earth science features that have formed our environment is part of learning biology (Philips, 1991).

 Activity: places where animals live

Make a list of the different biomes in the world such as desert, ice and snow, jungle, grasslands, woods, oceans. Repeat for geographical areas, for example, usually people say lions and tigers live in Africa, kangaroos live in Australia, camels live in deserts and dry hot places, polar bears live in snow and very cold northern areas. Make an 'animal I saw today' chart after watching a film or visiting a zoo. Perhaps the young scientist would like to draw the animal they saw that interested them the most?

A child's place

Children are born into this world into a place and environment, and immediately start developing a personal 'sense of place'. Through their gradual awareness of the immediate environment that knowledge and sense of place extends. In the beginning, the place is dependent on the Earth science of the planet manifest at this place. The first place is their home, and gradually the immediate outside becomes part of their environmental experiences, and the living things dependent on it, but they also learn about how the Earth, their part of our planet, is in their place. This understanding is formed by their early experiences.

Places have an identity. So, when beginning to learn about the living world, children under 3 years of age develop an understanding of the physical aspects, but also develop emotional, or affective, feelings towards it. Bradford (2012) was concerned with the developing child and understanding an appropriate environment. Although such developing understanding engenders a personal sense of place, this is often both the constructed and the natural environment.

Environmental education, however, tends to be focused on physical environments a child encounters, and to which they can be introduced to by educators and family as appropriate, to extend their experiences of 'place' and the varying environments that the places they frequent contain.

I understand 'nature' to mean 'the environment', in which most people think there is 'nature'. It is postulated nowadays that children are out of touch with nature. For example, Louv (2008) refers to a 'nature deficit' amongst these 'digitised' children, exposed to too much technology but not the untamed outside. However, even though urban children from an urban-focused society may have scant, if any, experience of wilderness, they have interactions with fauna, flora and Earth science in varying amounts, depending on what is found in 'their place' and, vicariously, through media. Hence, the natural environment, locations and components, as opposed to the built environment, is often the educational focus for environmental education. A large part of the environment that our children experience is the one constructed by humans. Hence, the built environment, the plundered, or that which is spoilt with non-biodegradable litter, is an important aspect of environmental awareness. Increasingly, the deleterious effect on the environment, where our own species has destroyed and has otherwise changed the landscape, has led to our era being named the Anthropogenic era (Scheersoi and Tunnicliffe, 2019). Some remedial actions are being taken because of heightened public and industrial awareness, such as recycling, in which many schools and communities encourage citizens to be involved in. There is little research on children's understanding of habitats. Anderson and Moss (2011) noted that infants' perceptions towards bogs and marshes were consistently more positive than those of juniors, whilst perceptions of woodlands improved with age. Perceptions of a variety of animals did not change with age and were as might be expected, lending credibility to the findings concerning habitats. The conclusion of these researchers is that conditioning leads to negative adult perceptions of wetlands. This conditioning may come from literature, television or orally, and it is not possible to rank these sources. However, a wealth of evidence does suggest that wetlands are negatively portrayed in junior and adult fiction but more positively in that written for infants. Teachers of juniors may thus have a key role to play in the conservation of wetlands by attempting, positively, to counteract the insidious influences of sources of misinformation.

The environment

The environment is the result of Earth science in action, both in the past and in the here and now. The soil, landscape, differing biomes and the differing vegetation, all contribute to the environment. Children have an understanding of vegetation (Harvey, 1989), which contributes to their understanding of their environment, and urban children have preferences for aspects of nature involving plants (Simmons, 1994). Young children notice habitats and their incumbents as well as noticing that the climate and weather effects all aspects of their environment (Moyle, 1980). However, with modern media they may become familiar with weather extremes such as typhoons, monsoons, floods and droughts, and these features vary depending on where the child is in the world (Wohlleben, 2012). Hence, environmental education embraces Earth science elements plus a living component and the remains of plants and animals. Much literature on environmental science emphasises the biological, not the physical or the Earth science. Young children experience the physical, outside world but do not remark upon it in their early vocabulary, which is particularly so in my son's case: rich in nouns and some verbs, such as 'dig', 'splash' (Tunnicliffe, 2013, p. 11). The natural environment of the Earth and sky and the built environment on the surface of the Earth is a large component of their 'place'. Japanese children experience the environment outside where they are able to observe things 'objectively and logically' (Sumida, 2013). Yet, other educators introduce nature journeys focusing on living organisms and not on the Earth science components such as soil, although these are essential for the emergence of the habitat, which are resultant of the climate of the area and which is, in turn, caused by the planet. Environmental education is thus more than nature education and provides real experiences for emergent scientists starting with their immediate surroundings.

Urban vegetable plots, known as allotments in some countries, act like urban jungles. They maintain the living world in towns and cities, which are otherwise mainly places of streets and buildings. Some citizens living amongst such concrete jungles campaign against these allotment areas, not realising they are vital for the sustainability of the planet (Rega-Brodsky, Hilson and Warren (2018)). Moreover, if children do not have the opportunity to explore and understand the living world, particularly in their everyday environment, there is little hope that the next generations of urban citizens will understand the need for such habitats.

Children's observations

Earth science awareness develops in children from their experiences and direct observations but, unless highlighted by a facilitator, it seems that it may become part of the background of 'place', although our emphasis is very much on the manifestation of the living world. The role of parents and other family members at home or teachers in nursery, childcare or play groups, as well as in the early years of formal school, is of utmost importance in helping these early learners develop their understanding beyond their personally generated ideas. Children look and think about their environment, and observe natural occurrences – e.g. sunrise, sunset, day and night (light and dark), beyond our planet into space – other worlds. Children observe change. In my experience, the sky and clouds catch the attention of the emerging environmentalist as do the weather patterns in their locality. The substrate under their feet is noticed if it is different! Young children have an inherent urge to collect items: pine cones, twigs or pebbles, or individual leaves (Tunnicliffe and Ueckert, 2011). They are also fascinated by wet soil and enjoy playing in mud, creating shapes and structures.

Henriques (2010), in a study of children's ideas about weather, held the belief that children do develop their own understanding of their everyday world and how it works before they are formally taught about it. However, most research was about physical sciences with very little of children's ideas about the Earth. Children interpret their world for themselves from what they notice, experience and hear, as borne out of a study by a group of researchers based at the University of Liverpool, UK, in the early 1990s, who investigated in a space project how young children developed an understanding of science (Russell et al., 1993).

On walks they appear fascinated by the content of the surface of the Earth, be it mud, sand, dusty soil, peaty soils, fined grained oil, clay, pebbles or pieces of rock, like chalk. In Japanese kindergartens, investigations of mud, usually with their hands, are facilitated by early years practitioners (Sumida, 2013). Children thus may learn to recognise where certain kinds of living things may like to live and where that kind would probably not live.

 Activity: bird watch

Is a bird always in the sky? Where have you seen birds on the ground?
How do they move on the ground? How many legs do they have? Do they move one leg after the other like you do when walking? What do you notice? Do some birds move both legs together and hop? Does how they move depend on where they live? Can you hop like a small bird that lives on the ground and hops short distances? What does it feel like? Easy? Difficult? Why do you think that?

Soil is vital for sustaining life. However, soil does not attract the attention of children if other eye-catching organisms are around, for instance unusual plants and moving animals. Indeed, there seems to be an acute 'Earth science blindness' (Tunnicliffe and Gkouskou, 2016) like that noticed by Wandersee and Schussler (1999, 2001). This is exemplified by my son's vocabulary as mentioned previously. He spent much time outside but experiences in his environment, his place, meant that he did not need to name the fundamentals – to him they were there for him to explore and to use, naming them was not important to him at this stage in his life.

We should remember that the term Earth is not a synonym for earth. Earth is the name of the planet while earth is its top covering (when not water) of soil, which comes in different forms depending on the bedrock from which it originated. As in the other sciences, children's ideas may conflict with the accepted scientific explanation. Remember the child's idea is what they have worked out for themselves from their experience and observations.

In the case of soil, it is a phenomenon that most children encounter when very young. Many children experience soil as an inert material containing, sometimes, dead bits. However, they also believe that soil is always brown and it is always the same wherever it is. Furthermore, some western children also think that it is constantly made because it can be bought in bags at special shops and has always been there. Recent works include that of Opperman et al. (2017), but there is relatively little research about Earth science beliefs. One of the most comprehensive is Book Number 7 of the SPACE (Science Processes and Concept Exploration) project (Russell et al., 1993). This was a large scale project that investigated primary school children's understanding of science. As in the other science topics, the researchers investigated the children's understanding of rocks and soil before they were given targeted teaching and the work showed that these children's ideas could be developed towards accepted science and that older primary children would understand rather more complex ideas than was hitherto believed. For instance, young children found it difficult to grasp the idea that rocks could break into smaller parts, but by the end of primary school (ages 9–11) nearly three-quarters of the children involved in the project could do so. Although weathering by water and the role of the sun was understood, the role of freezing and glaciation in times past, for example, was not grasped. The idea of time past is a challenge to children. However, the project could point out that if teachers knew their pupils level of understanding it would help considerably in their planning of the teaching and learning sequence. Earth is the name of our planet in the solar system where planets rotate around a central star, the Sun. Soil is a covering on many aspects of the planet in which plants grow.

 Talk science: the Earth beneath our feet

Ask what the word 'Earth' means to the children? Do they use it synonymously with soil? What is the difference between soil and Earth? Can they explain?

Activity: take an Earth walk

Ask a child: 'On what are you walking?' 'What is under your foot when you put it down?' Provide terms, such as stones, hard soil, gravel, mud, vegetation or grass, and other plants such as moss or buttercups. 'What can you see under your foot now?' 'Can you stand on one leg/foot and look at what was under the foot you lift up?'

'Is it the same under your other foot?' 'How could you find out?' 'Is it the same at your next step?' 'Is it the same if we move over there?' 'And over there?' 'Path or lawn, or whatever we are walking on?' 'What is under the grass plants in the lawn?' 'How could we find out?' 'What do the grass plants grow in?' Suggest solutions to your questions if the child does not answer. Listen to their explanations.

 Activity: feel the soil

On a walk collect several soil samples. Place them on a white surface, e.g. a small plate or a tray with a piece white paper on it (like a tissue or piece of kitchen towel). Are the soil samples the same? What can you see? Suggest to the child you pick up some of the soil together. A lollipop stick or plastic spoon can be useful for spreading out soil on the white surface so its constituents can be more easily seen. Young children usually have no qualms about using their bare fingers but some adults do and it does depend on the vicinity where you do this. Public areas, especially those visited by dogs, may have an infective organism in the soil, which a child should not ingest.

Soil is made from rocks. Some of the rocks forming your soil, may be amongst the pebbles you found. Chalky soils are most easily identifiable because they are lighter in colour than other soils and have small white pieces of chalk in them. Different kinds of plants live on different kinds of soil. Do you know what the soil around you is made of?

Soil affects the habitat

Soils and the climate of a place create specific habitats – pine trees, bracken, foxgloves and heather grow well on acidic soils in temperate climates, like our own here in the British Isles. Plants that need to conserve water, like cacti, grow in hot places with sandy soils, for example, in deserts where there is little rainfall. Sand dunes near the sea attract particular plants to grow on them, such as cord grass (*Spartina* sp.) and a type of ground-covering convolvulus. These sand-dune living plants must be able to tolerate a salty environment and survive on very few nutrients. Gardeners will tell you that roses like to grow on clay soils. Thus, the place or habitat where plants will grow depends on the soils and the climate. Scientists can predict what kinds of plants, and hence animals, are likely to live in certain places through observation of the environment.

Earth science 111

 Talk science: getting to know soil

What is your soil like? How can you tell? What colour is it? Is it all the same? Are there lumps in it? Or other things like twigs and stones? What plants grow well where you live? What do children suggest?

 Activity: sieving soil

Have a container in position under the sieve. What happens to the soil if you put it in a sieve? How can you find out? Children may suggest just spreading it out as before into a single layer. Talk about what happens, is anything in the container? Where have these bits come from? How? What happens if you use a sieve with bigger holes? Smaller holes? If our child just holds the sieve, ask them what else they could do to see if any bits would pass through the holes in the sieve, or move the sieve from side to side.

Rocks

The rocks in soil are small pieces that have been worn away from a large mass of rock, for example mountains, exposed to the atmosphere and roughened and eroded. Erosion is caused by the wind and by water, which fills the cracks then freezes, causing it to expand and then contract. Over many years this weakens the rock and causes pieces to fragment and break off.

 Talk science: ice

What can you make ice from at home? What do you need? Where do you make ice? Have you seen ice in puddles and ponds in the winter when it is very cold? What happens to the ice as the weather becomes warmer? How you can make ice at home?

 Activity: water to ice, ice to water – does it take up the same space?

What happens to water? How long does it take to make ice?
Does the ice look bigger in volume than the water you put in the ice-making container? What happens to the ice as it becomes warm? How can you find out?
Place some ice you have made in the container in which it was made.

> Does it fit? Leave it on top of the container, what do you think will happen? Why have you been asked to put it over the container in which the water was made into ice?

In the ice ages, rivers turned to ice which slowly moved downhill across the rocky surface of the river bed. As it moved slowly along, it took rocks and fragments with it, scraping and shifting rocks further along the river bed and carving out the valleys.

 Talk science: flows

Ask about floating something on a stream, watching how the item moves along from where it was put on the water. Have you ever done that?

 Activity: can a stream of water move things?

Have a tray as long as you can find and a small something that you know floats (or test the items to see what does, like a cork or a plastic bottle top or a very small bath toy). Find a jar or bottle that you can fill with water. Ask the child if by using water they can move the 'replica rock' from the end of the tray along it. What do they say? Try it their way and notice what happens. Try and work out a way to do this together. What do they say?

 Activity: erode some soil

Find a plastic tray and cover it with a thin layer of soil, along with a few small pieces of gravel or similar. Put your tray in a larger, deeper tray, with one end of the inner tray resting on the edge of the outer tray so it makes a slope (or make a slope another way). Place the trays on a waterpoof covering. Fill a container with water. It is most effective to use a small watering can fitted with a rose attachment at the end of the spout. Water the soil at the top of your slope in a line across. What do they think will happen? What does happen?

 Activity: how could you stop the erosion?

Listen to the children's suggestions on this – do the children propose putting things in the way of the water? Perhaps 'plant' twigs or lollipop sticks or small pieces of grass to simulate part of a grassy bank. What do they expect will happen? Do any methods help keep some soil on the slope you made? You may be able to find pictures of the effects of eroded slopes and solutions, such as planting trees on the slope to bind the soil with their roots and break the water flow with their trunks.

 Talk science: soil colours

What colours in the soil can you see? What other colours do you remember having seen? Have you looked at sand at the seaside?

Different soils – different places: habitats

Soil is not necessarily the same in one place as it is in another place. What we see around us is usually of a brown colour, but this is only the top of the soil. There are different layers beneath, right down until the bedrock is reached. Sometimes, if you see soil cut away as you do on river banks, you may see different layers and the top layer is usually darker. The colour of the topsoil depends on the sort of rock that it came from as well as the amount of water in it. It contains the remains of parts that were once living things, like plants and animals that live in the soil.

There are three main kinds of soils. They are sand, silt and clay. Most soils are composed of a combination of the different types. Soils are made of very small particles of the parent rock.

 Talk science: soil and size

Are all the parts of soil the same size? If the children have sieved the soil, what did they notice?

 Activity: particle size

If possible, obtain a spoonful of sand and one of clay and mix with your own soil if it is neither of these. Make sure the mixture is dry. How will you tell? What happens if you put it on a tissue – what would happen if the soil were wet?

Obtain a fine sieve. Ask the children to sieve the material by gently moving it from side to side. If some stays on the sieve, try stroking any lumps with a spoon. What happens? Examine the contents of the container, what do you see? Where has it come from?

114 Earth science

 Talk science: weigh me!

Ask the children if they think a spoonful of wet soil from the garden would weigh the same as a spoonful of dry soil. How could they find out? Design an investigation. What did you do? What did you find? What would happen if your soil were very wet? Much wetter than the normal soil you just used? Would it weigh more or less than the dry soil; more or less than the normal, garden soil? What makes the soil different? One thing has changed – what is it?

Pebbles

Pebbles means stones, shingle, grit or small rock. I have decided here to use the word pebbles. I will use the word rock a bit later on for deciding what kind of rock these small pieces came from originally – their geological identity.

 Talk science: pebbles

What can you see on the ground? Are there any pebbles? Can you look and say what they are all like? What colour are they? Are they alike in size? How do they feel in your hand? What kind of pebble do you find the most? How can you separate them so that in some way the same ones are together? Ask what feature of the pebbles they are using to decide whether they are the same or different.

 Activity: getting to know my pebbles

Take an example of each kind of pebble you have collected. Work with the child to try to describe them so their observations can be recorded, working like a scientist. Create an observation chart. Table 7.1 below could be useful to you.

Table 7.1 Collecting and observing pebbles

Pebble	Draw	Where found	Colour	Size	Feels like?	Other
Pebble 1						
Pebble 2						
Pebble 3						

Earth science 115

Rocks

We hardly notice the surface of the Earth beneath us except when it changes. Very young children, however, do notice it and investigate. Toddlers, in many parts of the world, like to play in dry silt, sand or mud. They delight in playing with these, scraping the dry soil up and pouring it into containers or making patterns in it.

 Talk science: rocks

You may notice larger stones with rough, jagged surfaces, unlike smooth stones or pebbles. These pieces have broken off from their 'parent' rock, much more recently than the soft, eroded pebbles, which have lost their jaggedness. Ask the children: are these like your pebbles? What is the same? What is different?

 Activity: give my rock a name

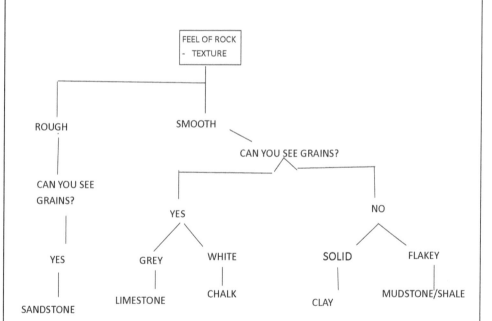

Figure 7.2 A simple rock identity chart

Collect some pieces of rock from the surface of the soil. Hold them to the chart given in Figure 7.2 and answer the questions. Where does your piece of rock fit? Try filling in this chart together.

116 Earth science

Weather

Weather is an important aspect of our lives. In some countries it is unpredictable yet with small variables, such as daily temperature within a small range, as well as rain and wind, as it is in the United Kingdom. In others parts of the world the seasons are more extreme and very distinct, for example, in monsoon season in Eastern Asia, or in desert conditions.

What does the word 'weather' mean to you and to a young child? Children experience weather because it affects them personally – what clothes do they wear for example in different kinds of weather? Do they need to take a raincoat to school every day? Do crops and garden plants need watering? Is there any water available or is there a drought because of little rainfall?

Talk science: what weather do you know ?

What kinds of weather do you know? What have you seen, or been in? Which sort of weather do you prefer? Why? How do you notice and know what the weather is each day? Do you wear the same clothes whatever the weather? Which weather do you like best? Why?

Activity: what I wear

Talk with the children about the kinds of weather they know. Ask them to talk about the clothes they wear for these different conditions, and why. Suggest types of clothes we wear in different weathers. Prepare a chart for the week. Draw a picture or a symbol of the kinds of weather each day and the clothes worn for that day, you can write down the children's comments! Talk together and try to fill in Table 7.2.

Table 7.2 The weather and what I wore

Day	Weather	What I wore	Why?

Young children try to predict the forthcoming weather by the clouds or the colour of the sky. They may have heard the saying 'Red sky at night, shepherd's delight, red sky in the morning, shepherd's warning'. Piaget (1929, p. 312) concluded that children's understanding of weather was restricted to sun, rain and wind. Children are often amazed at the strength of the wind if they try and stand or walk into it, and understand its power to move things through the air if they have, for example, a kite or have watched leaves blowing around. They also know that high winds often indicate a storm.

Children have varied explanations for the occurrence of rain and link it to clouds; some are convinced that the clouds are full of water and it is released through holes when it becomes too heavy (Philips, 1991). A 3-year-old girl I knew thought that condensation on the inside of windows was the rain coming in, as it had been raining outside when she announced this information. Piaget found that children believed that rain and clouds were not connected. Philips (1991) noted that another idea children held was that clouds are formed by boiling because it resembled the steam they saw from a boiling kettle (water vapour), or that the sun boiled the sea so the result went up in the sky as clouds. Henriques (2010) has written a comprehensive review of the literature of children's ideas of weather, clouds, air and the water cycle (Barr, 1989).

Talk science: weather

Is the weather the same every? How could you keep a record of the weather for a week? What weather do you all like best? Why? How would you record the weather – a drawing, a symbol or a word?

Activity: draw the weather

How could you draw the weather to explain to someone else who does not understand your language? Draw the current weather in a picture.

Activity: weather symbols

Can you show the weather by symbols? Which symbols would you use? Design your own symbol and say out loud why you chose that design, as outlined in Table 7.3.

Table 7.3 My weather symbols

Weather kind in my country	My drawing
Bright sun	
Overcast	
Storm clouds	
Hail	
Snow	
Thunder and lightning	
Storm winds	
Tsunami	
Light rain (drizzle)	
Fog	
Misty	

 Activity: act the weather

How can you explain the weather in noises and in miming? What actions can you do to show wind, sun, cloud, rain?

 Activity: our weather today

Draw a chart or use a printed calendar and record the weather you see in the morning. Note the time. How will you record your observations? Will you draw a weather picture or write about it?

Winds

Winds, when high, can be very frightening. Walking against a strong wind is difficult and you can feel the force of it pushing you back. Children notice twigs and branches on the branches, and even fallen trees when there have been very high winds. Apart from feeling the wind, children may have experience of flying kites or throwing light items into the air and watching them be tossed about in the wind.

Some 4-year-old children visiting ESPLORA, the exciting science centre in Malta, were fascinated by an air machine which blew air upwards and into the base of a column. They were able to put light pieces of cloth inside the column which were then were carried upwards and flew out of the top of the air tube. These children very excitedly collected up the pieces of fabric and put them back in the air column at the base of the tube.

 Talk science: wind force

How would you tell when wind was gentle, fast or strong? How do you tell when you look outside what kind of wind is blowing? What are the clues? Is it dead leaves and pieces of paper blowing around on the ground or in the air? Is it branches moving, is it washing on the line blowing about, or even your hair being ruffled? Children may have been given plastic or paper windmills on a stick, which whirl around when held in the direction of the blowing wind. Does the wind always blow from the same direction? Listen to what they say.

 Activity: which way is the wind blowing?

One old tradition is to wet your forefinger and hold it up to find out which direction the wind is blowing from. Try it! What happens to your wet finger? What could you suggest? Talk about how you could measure the strength of the wind.

Wind and living things

The wind is important to living organisms. It is one of the mechanisms used by plants in seed dispersal. When grasses or some other plants are in flower, some people suffer from hay fever. This unpleasant early summer ailment is an allergy. It is caused by the pollen of certain flowering plants like willow, grasses and birch trees. Wind pollination is one way for the male part of the plant to release its pollen to reach the female parts of another plant of the same kind. At certain times of the year, a light yellow dusting of pollen may be visible on cars and windowsills.

Sun

The clouds hide the sun, but it is always there. They will notice the changing position of the sun in the sky and they see it as alive (Venville, 2004), using the term 'the sun's out', or 'the sun has gone in'. Countries near the equator receive the most sun and here it is stronger and more intense than experienced in other places. When there is a lot of sun and little rain, the surface of the soil dries and regions called deserts are formed. Plants and animals that live there have adapted to life with little water and burrow to avoid the sun when it is very hot. Plants, like cacti, have leaves reduced to spines, as plants with large leaves lose water more rapidly. Plants with large leaves, therefore, live where there is much more water available for them.

Talk science: is the sun shining?

What parts of the world do you know of that are hot and dry? How can you tell when the sun is 'out'? How do you know that the sun is shining? What is different when there is no sun 'out'?

 Activity map: the sun

Take a large piece of paper and label the top left-hand corner 'Morning' and the top right 'Evening'. Ask the child to choose a lookout place and stand or sit there. Mark their place on the paper at the bottom of the page and ask them to draw the sun on the page in relation to where they are. Is it overhead or to one side? At the top of the page, middle way up or very near the bottom? Later in the day, return to the lookout place and sit/stand in the same place and observe where the sun is. Draw it. Carry on until the sun has disappeared. Look at a map of the world and talk about the different time zones.

When something in the sky covers the face of the sun it stops the sunlight reaching the Earth, so that surface does not heat up. As the sunlight weakens towards the end of the day, where the Earth's surface was warm, it is now cool. The reverse happens in the morning. Some cold-blooded animals, such as lizards, move very slowly when there is no sun and start their day by 'basking' in sunlight to warm up their bodies.

On the other hand, some animals actively hide in the daytime if they live in hot places, like deserts, and only come out when the sun has stopped shining and the Earth's surface has cooled. In a number of zoos, heated rocks are provided which attract animals like lions to sit and lie on them, so that visitors can view them. Hot air rises and, when the air is warm, birds take advantage of it and seem to soar effortlessly in the thermal currents. You may notice these phenomena by the edges of cliffs – seabirds, instead of using their wings to give them a 'push' and lift, use the hot air current instead.

Shadows

What makes shadows? If an object is opaque, that is, not see-through, the sunlight cannot pass through it, so behind the object, on the ground or something else like a wall, the shape of the object appears black. This is a shadow.

 Talk science: making shadows

Find a lamp or a torch and either a plain wall or make a screen. Switch on the lamp and face the screen or switch on the torch and point the beam at the screen. What does the screen look like? Put something in front of the beam of light and watch how it lights up the screen. What can you see? Use a book, a spoon or a cuddly toy. What happens to the front of your object when the light reaches it? What can you see on the screen? Is it like the screen was when you did not have something in the way? What can you see, does it look like the shape of anything? Why do you see that shape on the screen? What happens when you turn off the light? You have made a shadow.

Sun time-telling

In older times people made shadow clocks, called sundials. The time of day was indicated by the place the shadow fell on the dial, which was labelled with the hours of each day. They were not always very useful though – why?

 Activity: shadow shapes

Experiment with your hands to make shapes on the screen. Instructions for making various shapes, such as a rabbit's head, can be found on the internet. Shadows occur naturally. Can you talk about them? Where have you seen them outside? Can you make a shadow when outside? Can you do this every day or only on certain days? What do you need? Are shadows of the same object the same length all day whilst the sun is out? What do you think? How can you find out?

 Activity: design and make a shadow clock

You need a straight stick, soft ground and a piece of paper, together with a timer like a watch or a mobile phone set with an alarm for every time you want to observe where the shadow falls across the paper, and a marker. The easiest way is to place a stick upright in the ground and place pieces of paper (face down) around it and mark where the shadow falls every so often, perhaps every hour. What do you notice? Does the shadow stay in the same place? What do you think? Why do you say that?

Water

The sun heats the surface of the Earth, including any water lying on it. Wind also affects the water, and it disappears, sometimes quickly, sometimes slowly. Sometimes it seeps into the ground on soil or gravel. Children notice, often with glee, puddles and small areas of standing water. The combined effects of wind and sun cause shallow standing water, like puddles, to disappear by evaporation. Indeed, one small girl told her mother not to mop up her drink which she had knocked over and had formed a shallow puddle on the tiled floor, because it would soon disappear. Her mum still wiped up the fluid!

 Talk science: water

Have you seen water gradually disappear from the surface? Have you seen puddles? When? What is in puddles? Do puddles stay where you see them? Are they there the next day? What kind of weather do you think makes puddles?

 Activity: puddle shapes

Find a puddle. Draw around the edge with some playground chalk or place some string around its circumference. Anchor the string down with a few pebbles or other suitable items. Look at the puddle the next day. What has happened to the size of the puddle? Can you explain why? What has the weather been like since you outlined the puddle?

Animals hiding

Animals do not have clocks, but they can sense the time of day. Nocturnal animals sleep during the day and are active at night. Their eyes have adapted to see in the dark and they tend to have dark coats so they do not show up, a phenomenon which is known as camouflage. Some four-legged animals have counter shading; white underneath and darker on the top. This can be seen in antelopes which live in sandy places, like deserts and grasslands, their top coats appear to merge into the ground-covering colours. Other animals, like zebras, break up their body outline with stripes so that when they are gathered in a herd it is difficult for a predator to mark out a single animal. Other animals have very bright colours, usually red, which is a warning that they are poisonous. This can be seen in the venomous coral snake and other, similar snakes have evolved similar patterns and colours – they may be harmless but use their colour to confuse and warn possible predators.

 Talk science: feeling the Earth's surface

Talk about the surface of the Earth. Think about sand or soil, or paving. Do these surfaces always feel the same? Do the children ever walk on the Earth's surface in bare feet?

Night, moon and stars

As the planet rotates it moves away from the sun and light gradually disappears. The stars and the moon are seen in the sky instead. The moon also turns on its axis like the Earth, so when the moon is facing the sun, that side is brightly lit. We talk about the waxing of the moon as it becomes fully illuminated, and the waning as it appears to become less illuminated.

 Talk science: night sky

Have you seen the sky at night? What do you notice? Are the stars all as bright to look at as each other? What is the brightest thing you see? What different shapes can you see? Does the moon always have the same shape each time you look? What happens to it?

 Activity: moon shape

Suggest that you take photographs every week and see how the shape of the moon changes over five weeks. Alternatively, you could draw the sky on certain evenings for five weeks, making sure to include the shape of the moon.

Habitats

A habitat is where organisms live. The place where a person or other organism is usually found is their habitat. It has a climate, soil and plants to make the habitat, then it has the animals, which move in. Just as there are many different kinds of plants and animals, so it is with habitats.

Tapeworm and liver fluke adults for example, live inside larger vertebrates, often in the gut, and obtain their food from the host animal. These are called endoparasites. The ways in which their infective stage enters its host animal are varied. Tapeworms (*Taenia saginata* or *Taenia solium*), which are ones specific to humans, are eaten in meat, braclets (muscles), from infected pigs or cattle, which have eaten the eggs. These pass from humans in their faeces. Poor hygiene and sanitation means they can contaminate water. If an animal drinks this they may be infected. Humans can catch other kinds of tapeworms by eating tapeworm eggs in other uncooked foods. Another way of becoming infected is through an animal bite, whereby the eggs are passed into the victim's blood. The malaria parasite, for example, develops in the stomachs of some kinds of female mosquitoes and when she bites to obtain blood for food, the parasites pass into the bloodstream of the bitten human. Then the eggs are carried in the blood to where they develop into the adult form. Some parasites live on the outside of their host organism. These are called exoparasites, whereas animals living inside an animal, like parasitic worms, are called endoparasites. Fleas and ticks are exoparasites. Dogs and cats catch these exoparasites.

They may also catch worm endoparasites if they eat their prey or pick up worm eggs from the coats of other animals if they lick them. Plants have parasites too. My father grew Dodder plants from seeds in order to gain a series of photographs. Dodder (*Cuscuta* genus, belonging to the Convolvulus family) lives on the outside of another kind of plant. They have no roots and obtain all their food needs from their host plants. They are not green, thus cannot make their own food. Fungi also obtain all their nutrients from other living things; they are not plants.

Vegetation is made up of plants. Children have an understanding of vegetation, which contributes to their understanding of their external environment. Simmons (1994) commented that urban children have preferences for aspects of nature involving plants, but gradually adopt the adult attitude that vegetation is worthless and utilitarian (Schneekloth, 1989). Children learn about plants from their family, be it someone trying to eradicate moss from the lawn, planting out flower beds, hanging baskets or just admiring specimens seen on walks or in the media, as well as learning a lot from their own everyday observations. A study eliciting an understanding of plants and animals amongst young children in the USA and England (Patrick and Tunnicliffe, 2011) found that the children were in touch with their everyday environment.

Early years children experience this 'plant blindness'. My own observations of primary school children visiting botanical and horticultural gardens is that they are interested in plants until they are distracted by an animal moving (Wandersee and Schussler, 1999). 'Plant' is a term restricted in everyday understanding to refer to the small herbaceous Angiosperms, also referred to as flowers (Ryman, 1974). Bell (as Stead, 1980) found that children aged 9–15 had a much narrower meaning of the word plant than biologists. A tree for example is not considered to be a plant and everyday grouping of plants, such as weeds, vegetables and seeds, were considered equivalent categories to 'plant' not subsets. Early years children (4 year olds), when interviewed about everyday plants (unpublished data), used the word 'grass' as synonymous with the stretch of green called a lawn and when shown, firstly, an individual grass plant from a lawn and, secondly, a mature grass plant in flower, were amazed. Plants are an important background part of children's lives. Their plant experiences begin in their home with indoor plants and plant parts, such as apples and other fruits, the leaves of cabbage and the seeds of some legumes (peas and beans).

Animals, in the home or outside, have an important part in a child developing an understanding of environmental science. Indeed, the naming of whatever is noticed is the beginning not only of language capability but also the beginning of scientific skill acquisition and understanding – it is the beginning of the child's science capital.

Formally learning about places, its constituent parts and the effects of the environment, the rocks and soils, the climate and the habitats formed on the environment, are a key aspect of learning about the living world. Without the planet, the soils and the climate, there would be no living things. The Earth came first. Without green plants, which depend on the soil and associated Earth science aspects, there would be no animals. A holistic view of the environment in which you and your children are living is very important so that you recognise and are able to encourage them to save the world and keep it sustainable, in which organisms, including all of us, live.

Talk science: places to live

Animals live in the habitats which suit them. What is your habitat? What different places for plants and animals to live can you see where you are? Where would you expect a polar bear to live? In a forest or grassland? In a desert? Places such as under stones where the sun cannot reach, what do you think it is like there? Hot, sunny, wet, cold and windy? Have you noticed which animals do live there? Do plants live under stones?

 Activity: plants under a stone

Choose a small piece of lawn of grass plants and notice what colour the plants are. Cover the small area with something through which light will not pass, like a stone or bowl. Leave it for a few days. When you take off the cover what can you see? What did you stop reaching the grass plants by covering them?

 Talk science: in the shade

What would it feel like in a damp place? Would the place receive much sun? How can you tell? Can you find a wall that is out of the sun, in the shade? Are there any plants growing there?

Understanding the system of the Earth and how living things depend on these is vital for children to begin to learn, in this anthropogenic age, where the deleterious effects of human activity, particularly from the developed and developing world, have such devastating effects on the planetary systems. Mega fauna, the 'Noah's Ark' animals such as elephants and rhinoceri, are predicted to become extinct in the 21st century if action is not taken by humans. It is not just these well-known animals but smaller, boneless ones on which plants depend, for example for pollination before fruits, such as grains, are produced. Honey bees are threatened because of some weed killer chemicals, whilst rivers, such as the Danube in Germany, are heavily polluted with oath hosing antibiotics. This high incidence in these waters may be contributing to the antibiotic resistance in many bacteria, which cause serious illness in humans and others. However, efforts are now increasingly being designed and implemented to mitigate some of these deleterious effects. Environmentalists are rewilding areas, not with the species that once lived there, but an equivalent organism, which has the same effect on the environment. After rewilding, some animals are returning, like the White Stork (*Ciconia ciconia*) to the east of England, to breed after centuries of non-appearance. Efforts to clean up the pollution in the River Thames, which flows through London, have helped in the reappearance of salmon, but pollution, although now much reduced, is still found in the water. Children are becoming increasingly aware of these issues and want to take action. But first they must understand the dynamics of the Earth's systems and their interactions.

Conclusion

Our planet Earth, and its structure, has a profound effect on our lives and that of other living things in a variety of ways. An understanding of climate, soils, land features and their interrelationships are vital to understand the living world, but this aspect of scientific learning has not been fully explored in the teaching of early years children. Furthermore, the role of biological conservation in preserving habitats, for which the conservationist requires a sound understanding of the environment and the needs of the organism, is also overlooked.

 Activity: animal snap

Make animal snap cards. Use pictures of animals cut from magazines or downloaded from the internet. Play snap, naming each animal as you place it down. Do you know where such animals live naturally? Are they endangered? How can you find out?

Through the activities suggested in this chapter, children, as emergent biologists, may begin to grasp the importance of not studying animals and plants in isolation, but within the ecosystem of which they are an integral part. If organisms and habitats experience destruction, by extreme weather, catastrophic natural events or by another species, the delicately balanced ecosystem often collapses. An understanding of the geological origins of ecosystems, the particular habits of organisms and the weather patterns generated by the planet, is vital for conservation biologists to understand the conditions a species requires and the effects of changes in those parts of the interlinked system.

References

Anderson, S. and Moss, B. (2011) How wetland habitats are perceived by children: consequences for children's education and wetland conservation. *International Journal of Science Education*, 15(5): 473–485. DOI: 10.1080/0950069930150502.

Arthus-Bertrand, Y. (2008) *Our Living Earth. A Next Generation Guide to People and Preservation*. London: Thames & Hudson.

Balmer, D. (2018) Advancing science, improving education. In Costa, M.F.P.C.M., Dorrío, J.B.V. and Novell, J.M.F. (eds), *Hands-on Science, Advancing Science, Improving Education*. Braga: Hands-on Science Network, pp. 235–240.

Barr, V. (1989) Children's views about the water cycle. *Science Education*, 73(4): 481–500.

Bradford, H. (2012) *Appropriate Environments for Children under Three*. Abingdon, UK: Routledge.

Harvey, M. (1989) Children's experiences with vegetation. *Children's Environmental Quarterly*, 6(1): 36–43.

Henriques, L. (2010) Children's ideas about weather: a review of the literature. *School Science and Mathematics*, 102(5): 202–215. DOI: 10.1111/j.1949-8594.2002.tb18143.x.

Leach, J., Driver, R., Scott, P. and Wood-Robinson, C. (1996) Children's ideas about ecology 3: ideas found in 5–16 about the interdependency of organisms. *International Journal of Science Education*, 18(2): 129–141. DOI: 10.1080/0950069960180201.

Louv, R. (2008) *Last Child in the Woods*. Algonquin: Chapel Hill.

Medin, D., Waxman, S., Woodring, J. and Washinawatok, K. (2010) Human-centeredness is not a universal feature of young children's reasoning: culture and experience matter when reasoning about biological entities. *Cognitive Development*, 25(3): 197–207.

Moyle, R. (1980) *Weather*. Learning in Science Project (Working Paper 21). Hamilton: University of Waikato, New Zealand.

Oppermann, E., Brunner, M., Eccles, J. and Anders, Y. (2017) Uncovering young children's motivational beliefs about learning science. *Journal of Research in Science Teaching*, 55(3): 399–421.

Patrick, P. and Tunnicliffe, S.D. (2011) What plants and animals do early childhood and primary students' name? Where do they see them? *Journal of Science and Educational Technology*, 20(5): 630–642.

Philips, W.C. (1991) Earth science misconceptions. *The Science Teacher*, 58(2): 21–23.

Piaget, J. (1929) *The Child's Conception of the World*. London: Routledge & Kegan Paul.

Rega-Brodsky, C., Hilson, C. and Warren, P.S. (2018) Balancing urban biodiversity needs and resident preferences for vacant lot management. *Sustainability*, 10(5): 1679. DOI: 10.3390/su10051679.

Russell, T., Longden, K., McGuigan, L. and Bell, D. (1993) *Rocks, Soil and Weather*. Liverpool University Press – Primary SPACE Research Reports. Liverpool: Liverpool University Press.

Ryman, D. (1974) Children's understanding of the classification of living organisms. *Journal of Biological Education*, 8: 140–144.

Scheersoi, A. and Tunnicliffe, S.D. (2019) Foreword. In Scheersoi, A. and Tunnicliffe, S.D. (eds), *Natural History Dioramas – Traditional Exhibits for Current Educational Themes. Socio-cultural Aspects*. Cham: Springer, p. 1.

Schneekloth, L.H. (1989) "Where did you go?" "The forest." "What did you see?" "Nothing.". *Children's Environmental Quarterly*, 6(1): 14–17.

Simmons, D.A. (1994) Urban children's preferences for nature: lessons from environmental education. *Children's Environments*, 11(3): 194–203.

Stead, B. (now Bell) (1980) *Plants. LISP Working Paper 24*, Science Education Research Unit, Hamilton: University of Waikato.

Sumida, M. (2013) The Japanese view of nature and its implications for the teaching of science in the early childhood years. In Georgeson, J. and Player, J. (eds), *Perspectives on Early Childhood and Care Education*. Maidenhead, UK: Open University Press, pp. 242–256.

Tunnicliffe, S.D. (2013) *Talking and Doing Science in the Early Years. A Practical Guide for Ages 2–7*. Abingdon, UK: Routledge.

Tunnicliffe, S.D. and Gkouskou, E. (2016) HSCi physical science learning opportunities at natural history dioramas. In Costa, M.F.P.C.M., Dorrío, J.B.V., Trna, J. and Trnova, E. (eds), *Hands-on : The Heart of Science Education*. Braga: The Hands-on Science Network, pp. 1–9.

Tunnicliffe, S.D. and Reiss, M.J. (2000) Building a model of the environment: how do children see plants? *Journal of Biological Education*, 34: 172–177.

Tunnicliffe, S.D. and Ueckert, C. (2011) Early biology: the critical years. *Journal of Biological Education*, 45(4): 173–175.

Unsworth, S.J., Levin, W., Bang, M., Washinawatok, K., Waxman, S.R. and Medin, D.L. (2012) Cultural differences in children's ecological reasoning and psychological closeness to nature:

evidence from Menominee and European American children. *Journal of Cognition and Culture*, 12 (1–2): 17–29.

Venville, G. (2004) Young children learning about living and things: a case study of conceptual change from ontological and social perspectives. *Journal of Research in Science Teaching*, 41(5): 449–480.

Wandersee, J. and Schussler, E. (1999) Preventing plant blindness. *The American Biology Teacher*, 61: 4–86.

Wandersee, J. and Schussler, E. (2001) Towards a theory of plant blindness. *Bulletin of Botanical Society of America*, 47(1): 2–8.

Wohlleben, P. (2012) *The Weather Detective: Rediscovering Nature's Secret Signs.* (trans.) Ruth Ahmedzai Kemp. London: Rider.

Chapter 8

Interactions between physical science and living things

Introduction

As humans we are part of the living world along with all the various other organisms, presently classified into six kingdoms and divided further by cell numbers and structure. Physics is another domain to which we do not belong in the same way as we do to the biological one, but we use many of the concepts of it in our structures and functions, as do other animals. Hence, it is important to be familiar with how they are present in us and other animals. Vogel (2009) reminds us that organisms exist in a physical world and even though evolution through natural selection occurs, it does so within this physical context, which exists on our Earth.

This physical context, which has limitations yet also opportunities, is the baseline of the existence of living things. Hence, an awareness of physical science, even at a basic level as introduced in this chapter, is an important stage for learners.

This chapter focuses mostly on animals, largely mammals, as they are much more a part of a young child's experience, especially because they move and attract the attention of early learners; plants are more usually seen as an accessory to their observations.

This chapter revisits the idea that while plants do not move from place to place, parts of them do. Plants utilise many physical phenomena such as capturing light energy to make food, standing upright, bending yet not breaking off in wind and remaining firmly rooted in the soil with roots extending in a wide circumference below the ground to increase anchoring power. Some simple activities with seeds are suggested. Physics in action is noted in animals, including humans, which young children can observe and may notice spontaneously. Some simple activities are suggested that have been used many times with learners (Tunnicliffe, Gazey and Gkouskou, 2015).

Moving plants

Whole plants do not move around by themselves from place to place as do most animals, however, they do have movements other than locomotion. Some parts of them grow and thus move upwards but stay rooted in the same place whilst they grow. Certain other plants, like blackberries or strawberries, grow stems outwards across the ground and root in the soil when a new plant will grow there. Some plants or their seeds are blown by the wind and move to new places, others are carried by animals who may eat them and excrete them somewhere away from the parent plant in their droppings, where a new plant can then grow.

 Talk science: moving seeds

Have you planted a seed? Where did you put it? Can you see it once you have planted it? Why not? How do you know the seed is developing then? What do you see?

Let's plant some seeds, what do you think will happen? Does anything move?

 Activity: moving parts!

You need a small, see-through container with some kitchen towel or similar in, some fast-growing seeds (e.g. chickpeas) and some water. Soak the seed until it is not wrinkly any more. Put some seeds in the container between the wall of the container and the kitchen towel so it (or whatever you use) keeps them in place next to the see-through wall. Make a mark on the outside of the see-through container with a washable marker or stick a label down the length of the container side and mark where the seed is. Make sure the paper is kept moist. Watch the seed every day.

Has anything grown so you can see it? Which way is it growing? Mark how far this grows each day. Does anything grow from the opposite end of the seed, in a different direction? Mark when anything else appears and how far it moves.

 Talk science: what comes out of seeds?

Which parts of a plant do you know of that will have to grow from the seed?

Which way does the root grow? Which way does the shoot grow? Which way do leaves grow? Do all leaves on all kinds of plants grow in the same direction?

 Activity: upside down

Repeat the above activity. Try planting some seeds in the same way but upside down. Which way does the root grow now, which way did the shoot grow? Why? Towards gravity or away from gravity?

Roots grow downwards under the effect of gravity, but shoots grow upwards to the light. Plants do have moving parts, but they move relatively slowly.

Plants grow towards the light. You can try this by putting, for example, a sprouting potato in a box with a hole at one end. Cover the box, only taking off the lid to look at it once a day.

Some flowers, such as spring crocus, open in the sunlight but close when the sun sets. Seedpods may suddenly explode if touched, spreading the seeds widely, for example, *Impatiens* or 'Busy Lizzie'. In others, a leaf will move suddenly; the leaves of a mimosa tree will close the two halves to meet when touched, while the leaves of a carnivorous Venus fly-trap will close over an insect that lands on part of the leaf, after which the animal is digested.

Movement of animals

Movement is one of the characteristics of animals and pre-secondary children, and often adults, cite it as the defining one. Most animals can make some observable movement and most possess the power of locomotion, being able to move from place to place at some point in their life. This locomotion has many functions such as food finding, escaping, hunting, finding a mate, running and walking. The mover pushes against something – water, land or air.

Talk science: moving you

What part of your body do you use to 'push' against the ground to make you move along when walking? Running? Swimming? What would you push against if you could fly? What would you use to push? Can you think of an animal that does this while moving through the air? What does it use to push? What about an animal that lives in water? What do they do to move? What do they push against? What parts of their body does the pushing?

Activity: walk in slow motion

Take a step, freeze! What does that mean? What have you done? Which part of your body have you used? Now what do you do to move forwards having taken this first step? Slowly take the action of your next step. What do you do? Which part of your body do you use? What happened to your torso (the body to which your leg is attached)? Does it stay in the same place? Does it lean at all – forwards, backwards, to the side?

Freeze! What does that mean? Now you have moved your body forwards, what do you have to do with the first leg, which is still on the ground? Have you moved forwards?

What did you do to leg one? What did it feel like?

132 Physical science and living things

In touch with the ground

You cannot walk around unless you have something on which to walk, to push against. When walking, a part of the body is always touching the ground and when running, there is a time when the body is out of contact with the ground. The same applies to four-footed animals when walking. When the first leg swings through to put its foot forward, it acts like a pendulum. This is the principle of human walking: the pendulum.

 Talk science: pendulum

Have you ever swung a piece of string with a blob of play dough on the end you are not holding? Shall we? What do you think will happen? Why do you think that?

Animals moving

The mechanisms of propulsion in swimming animals are that of the propeller, the oar, jet propulsion and body undulation. Children learn quickly how fish and penguins move in water if they have been able to see the animals in action, in real life in an aquarium or through the media.

Penguins are not fish, they are birds (whales, dolphins and porpoises are not fish either, they are mammals and come to the surface of the water in which they live to breathe). Penguins spend much of their time swimming under the water. They use their wings as hydrofoils, a surface that lifts and so moves them up and down, whereas rowers like water spiders use their limbs like oars, moving them backwards and forwards. Penguins are not very effective walkers on land – they waddle.

Many fish 'row themselves' using their fins, especially when swimming slowly. Whales propel themselves by up and down movements of their tail fin flukes and some fish, like trunkfish, move their tails from side to side, not up and down. Some animals such as eels, leeches and water snakes, swim using a movement like the snake uses on land. Seahorses use their fins in a wave-like motion; cuttlefish, relatives of octopi, swim slowly by undulation and fast by jet propulsion. All movement is through the action of a force pushing against something that pushes back (resists) or doesn't 'give' when you push against it.

 Activity: pendulum

Try swinging a pendulum. You need a piece of play dough or you can tie a washer fixed to the end of a piece of string about 20 cm long. This is the bob. Hold the end of the string without the bob in your hand. Swing the piece of string forwards and backwards in a straight line. What happens to the bob? Where does it go? Will the string act in the same way without a bob? Why not? What does it do when you swing it?

Activity: walking with your pendulum

The bob repeatedly rises and falls and slows down and speeds up. As the bob swings down, it loses height and thus potential energy; when it rises up it gains height and kinetic energy. Energy is swapped backwards and forwards. In walking, the person slows down and rises in the first half of each step but speeds up and falls in the second half – try it!

Our power source for moving upright across the surface is our leg muscles. Muscles produce the power that start off the leg swing and can give the leg pendulum a boost if needed or slow it down. Watch as one leg acts like a pendulum and swings under your body until your foot is on the ground in front of your body. When one leg is on the ground the other moves, swinging through until that foot touches the ground. Then this leg swinging sequence starts again, and again, and again, resulting in the movement of walking.

Leg muscles have to give a boost to the walking at one stage (increasing the mechanical energy of the body) and act like a brake at other times (converting mechanical energy to heat). The principal of running is that of a bouncing ball. Many bounces are made without an input of energy. In human running, the Achilles tendons in the legs give that bounce.

All the movements that push against a surface depend on their pushing part being able to 'get a grip' and not slip. Friction is when one thing stops another from moving, like a non-slip mat or your foot pushing against a rough surface. Then there is resistance to one object moving relative to another. When there is little or no resistance you slide!

 Talk science: to slip or not to slip?

How do you manage to push forwards when your foot is on the floor? What happens on a slippery floor and your foot cannot get a grip? When have you slipped? On what were you walking?

 Activity: to grip or not to grip

Try answering the questions by doing the actions. Take care when trying to slip. Have an adult hold you or use the back of a chair to support you so that you do not fall.

> **Talk science: stopping!**
>
> If you roll a ball along a floor does it keep rolling for ever? Not usually, because the ball runs out of the energy that was given to it by the initial propulsive action. It loses momentum as it moves over the surface, and that uses energy. A challenge: how can you stop something moving, like a toy car you push off to move across a floor? What does the emergent scientist say?
>
> Can they devise an investigation to find ways of stopping a toy car running across a smooth surface? Suggest ideas, such as putting a wooden block in its path or place it on another kind of surface like a mat or a piece of cloth. Trying the same investigations outside can be interesting. What surfaces do they themselves find more difficult to walk over because they can be a little slippery and what surfaces give them a good grip so they are less likely to slip?
>
> Have they any advice to give to other people about the kind of footwear that is advisable to use when walking on different surfaces?

> **Activity: how do I stop the moving toy**
>
> What does the child think they could do? What is their hypothesis? What do they say they already know which makes them think that? What do they need? What is the plan? What will they do? What measurements will they take – distance? Time? What do they say when they have carried out the investigation?

Think about how animals move and how to solve the problem of slipping and sliding, starting and stopping.

Flight in birds

When wind passes over a curved surface, like a bird or aeroplane wing, the wind moves more quickly over the rounded surface on top than it does over the flat surface underneath. This movement over the two surfaces causes lift. When aeroplanes take off, they need to be moving fast along the runway so that they can achieve sufficient power for lift-off. Birds have to do the same. As they run along the ground, or water, they also flap their wings until they lift off. When an aeroplane lands, it puts brakes on the wheels, drops the power, putting the engine into a reverse thrust, and raises parts of the wing called spoilers which stick up and stop air flowing over it, acting like a brake. Birds do the same kinds of actions. As they land, they put their body more upright and stick out their feet more, spread their wings and touch the ground with their feet, heel first. It is dramatic to watch birds such as swans landing on water. Some birds launch themselves into the air from the tops of trees or high buildings, they use their wings, pushing down against the air by flapping up and down like a 'motor' until they become caught by a current of wind. Birds of prey and seabirds do this as they search for food on land or sea.

 Talk science: take-off

Have you ever seen a bird running to take off? Watch and note what they do. What does it do as well as run? Have you seen any birds fly into the air from standing still on the ground? Have you ever felt the force of the wind blow you from upright or have another effect on you, your hat or your umbrella?

 Activity: paper lift

You need a piece of A4 paper, not too stiff nor too light. Hold it with both hands either side of the paper at the end in front of your mouth. Hold the paper so it is almost touching you. Blow out across the top of the paper. Does anything happen to the other end of the paper, which is flopping down? You have lifted the paper with your air blow!

All birds, except flightless ones such as rheas and ostriches, fly in the same basic way, but the operation may differ. Small birds tend to hover a little before landing rather like helicopters, whereas larger birds, like seagulls, fly flapping their wings, but when coming into land they 'switch off power' then glide and lower their legs, like the undercarriage of an aeroplane as it gradually reaches the ground.

Water birds have to run on the surface of the water to take off like an aircraft. They must move faster and faster along a runway until they achieve lift and then take off. When landing, water birds descend on a gradual slope. Near the surface of the water they spread their wings like spoilers being raised on an aircraft wing and put their feet out at right angles to the water, which allows them to slow down. This movement is particularly noticeable in swans.

When you or other animals move there has to be some power produced from somewhere. Vehicles need a source of power such as petrol, or increasing electricity, to make the motors produce enough power to make them move. The power has to provide energy to make the muscles work by pushing or pulling on animals and their skeletons. When the movement happens, the energy for the muscles to work comes from our food.

Skeletons

Skeletons can be inside the animal's body (internal) or outside (external), or it may retain fluid inside the body as a waterproof cover (hydrostatic skeleton), such as you would see in an earthworm or jellyfish.

136 Physical science and living things

Forces which initiate movement are provided by contraction of the muscles – striated and smooth (voluntary and involuntary), and they move the internal organs or limbs and other appendages, your legs. Muscles act on skeletons and skeletons are made of bone (70 per cent) calcium phosphate crystals embedded in a protein called collagen (30 per cent). This mixture of composite structure crystals plus a protein is important. Without the protein the skeleton would be too brittle, but protein alone would be too weak. Bone and insect cuticle is as stiff and strong as hardwood. Children gradually learn that they have an internal skeleton (their ideas are discussed in Chapter 2). Few children talked about muscles in the research work we carried out (Reiss and Tunnicliffe, 2001).

It is useful to talk about muscle action with early learners because they can feel their own muscles working. As they tighten, muscles shorten. Relaxing muscles produces lengthening. Each muscle has one that acts as its opposite – when one shortens and pulls the other is relaxed and vice versa. The elbow is bent and straightened through the action of the biceps and triceps – an antagonistic muscle pair. If the animal has a hydrostatic skeleton, e.g. an earthworm, the animals have a circular layer and a longitudinal layer of muscles which squeeze it thin and then make the next part fat and hence move the body along – the muscles work by pressing on fluid which is incompressible inside the animal's body. The animal gets thinner and longer, shorter and fatter. Fluid is incompressible, so it makes an excellent base for muscles to push against. Bending of the animal is caused by contracting the longitudinal muscles on one side while keeping the circular muscles the same length. The bristles on the underside of the fat segment stick into the surface the work is on and then this pulls the worm forwards. Snakes have a backbone, which cannot be compressed. They contract the muscles on one side and stretch the muscles on the other to move. They press against the ground making waves to pass down their body as they move forwards.

 Talk science: bending

Have you felt what happens under your skin in your upper arm as you bend your elbow up? What do you think that is? Have you ever seen a string puppet or marionette moving? How do they move? What makes their arms and legs move? Who is providing the energy for that? Have you ever seen a jellyfish moving in water? If so, what do you notice? Have you seen a bird fly? What do they use to do this? What do they push against? What about fish? What about a dog?

 Activity: move a card arm!

First, draw a cardboard arm. You will need card from a cereal box, a screw, split pin or drawing pin/panel pin and something to pin onto, sticky tape, a hole punch and a ruler. Cut out two pieces of card, each piece about 20 cm long and 3 cm wide. You could cut them into a bone shape with curves at each end. How can they be placed and fixed together to look like an arm and to stay together?

Names of the limb bones

In reality the lower part of a vertebrate limb – arm or leg – has one bone in the upper part (the humerus in the arm or the femur in the leg), and two smaller straight bones below the limb joints (the elbow in the arm and the knee in the leg).

The two bones in the lower leg are the tibia and the smaller one, the fibula. In the arm the larger lower arm bone is the ulna and the smaller one the radius. This is the basic vertebrate pattern. In some vertebrate animals, such as fish, the bones are cartilaginous as in baby mammals before they are born. Bones develop from cartilage *after* birth. The limbs end at the wrist and anklebones, named the tarsals in feet and the carpals in arms. These bones allow the arm or leg, hand or foot, to make circular, rotating movements. The main bones of hands and feet are called metatarsals (feet) and metacarpals (hands). At the ends are the digits, toes or fingers, which are made of small bones, the phalanges.

 Activity: can you make an arm with a moving elbow?

Take the two pieces of card and pin the two pieces down carefully on a hard surface. Pierce a hole through both ends of the card where they meet, so that each piece will move. If you tie the two pieces together with string, that also works. If you prefer, just pin the two pieces together using a drawing pin. You'll need to do this on a cork mat, craft mat or a thicker piece of card. The drawing pin should act as a pivot. What happens if you hold down one end of one piece of card and push the end of the other one? Does the movement remind you of any action you do with your arm? Where does your arm pull from? Is it near the elbow or further away? Where did you pull the card to make the pieces move?

 Activity: make your model arm bend and unbend

Experiment as to where the most effective place is to pull up your card 'forearm'. You can fix the string on the arm with pieces of adhesive tape. When you try to bend the 'arm' pull the other end up in the same direction as the upper 'arm' card. Which position is most successful for a pull to work the best? Once you have made a model of the muscles that bend your arm, how can you unbend it again? Where do you need to attach the unbent muscles to the model arm? Experiment and see. Can you feel these muscles on yourself and feel your muscles working to move and then straighten your arm?

138   Physical science and living things

 Talk science: no bend!

How do you think an animal like a beetle with a hard shell manages to move? How do you move? What happens if you hurt your knee and cannot bend it?

What do you do with your leg? How do you walk? Have you any idea of how an animal with a hard outside could make its legs bend?

 Activity: your skeleton

Can you draw a stick line skeleton on a sheet of paper? Now you have looked at limbs, where do the children think there are other bones? Can you feel them on yourselves? What do they say? Can you draw what they say? Use sticky notes or small pieces of paper and then try fitting them together like a basic jigsaw.

 Talk science: keeping your head on your body

Most children realise there is a bone around their head, a skull. Draw a squashed circle. Ask if there is anything else attached to the skull which moves (and don't forget teeth, they don't move and are inside the mouth). Children usually work out that they have a jawbone, so draw that.

Ask them: Where does the skull (head) attach to the rest of the body? To what do the arms and leg attach? Can you feel where on yourselves? The shoulder blades and the hips form the pectoral and pelvic girdles. Where do limbs attach to the girdle? Where does the girdle attach to the spinal cord?

Research carried out by Reiss and Tunnicliffe (2001) found that children learn about skeletons from starting to know about bones and gradually learning that these group together in 'bone units', like arm bones, leg bones, ribcages, which eventually join up to make the whole skeleton. An understanding of the two bones in the lower arms and legs appears after realising there are two parts to limbs (in fact, three parts counting hands and feet). They do not learn from being shown a complete skeleton first.

 Activity: skeleton jigsaw

Find some scissors and a drawing or photograph of a complete human skeleton. Photocopy or scan it so you have two copies of it then cut one of the copies up into its individual bones. Ask the emergent scientist if they can piece them together. You could try the same activity using pictures of cat, dog or fish skeletons.

Once children have understood the idea of bones being joined together to form the skeleton, try making your own skeleton model!

 Activity: build a card or paper skeleton

Cut out basic shapes making the skeleton model in flat card and join with a punched hole and string, or treasury tags through the punched holes so that the cardboards limbs move. Staple, tape or glue the representations of the spinal column, pelvic girdle and ribs, as they do not move much. Make sure you make your 'bones' the real proportions. The leg bones are longer than the arm bones and the upper arm and upper leg bones are longer than the lower arm and leg bones. Most skeleton makers only put one bone below the knee, in the lower limb and cut out a basic hand and foot shape for the appendages. A straight roll of paper to which the limbs are attached represents the pectoral and pelvic girdles. The skull can be a blown-up round balloon or a cut-out circle.

Attach the whole model to a wire coat hanger and hang it up! Some children like to name the bones too.

Crawling

Some animals without legs can move – how do they do this? Earthworms have pairs of chaetae or bristles on the skin which cover each segment. The fluid cannot be squashed so acts like a bone skeleton. This firm base also acts like a ratchet and anchors the animal to the ground as it pulls the body up while contracting its muscles. If you find an earthworm in the soil, carefully place it on a piece of paper and listen to the chaetae scratching the paper as it moves along. Make sure you return the animal to where you found it as soon as you have listened. Or if you have any mealworms (see Chapter 3, p. 37) you can place them on your hand and feel them pulling themselves across the surface of your skin.

Snails and slugs crawl along using their muscular foot covered in slimy mucus. The muscular foot contracts and slides along. The mucus acts, for land crawlers, like a ratchet. If it is pressed hard enough the mucus stops acting like a solid and gives way so that the animal moves on. The pressure from the muscular foot, which is contracting and pushing forwards, is such that the mucus is liquefied. Thus, when the body is extended the mucus is liquefied but when it is contracted it is rigid. You may be able to see this as a slug or snail moves. Placing a slug or snail on a transparent sheet of plastic and looking up at the underneath of the foot of the snail or slug enables you to see this in action. This may also be seen in water living molluscs in aquaria. If you see a water snail on the side of a glass aquarium you can see the waves of muscles as they contract and relax on the foot as the animal moves across the glass. You may notice its mouth opening and closing as it eats algae on the glass.

Mass and balance

Every object or living thing on our planet has a mass. We notice this in what we call 'weight'. If you were able to visit another planet, such as Mars, our mass would be of a different value. Astronauts walking in space experience weightlessness because there is no gravity. Gravity stops our planet spinning off into space. Some science centres have weighing machines on which you can weigh yourself as if you were on Mars for example. The value of the mass depends on the strength of the gravitational pull of that planet. Mass is the amount of matter an object has. Our centre of mass is important for us so that we can stay upright and move but balance also applies to other living things. If you think about your balance there is one position when you are standing up when you are balanced, otherwise you would fall over. If you move from that position you will fall over unless you change it.

 Talk science: spreading the body load

Camels live on sand and have wide feet to spread the load of their weight over a larger surface area so that they do not sink. This is similar to a human wearing snowshoes when travelling across snow. Other animals that live on soft ground, like the Sitatunga (*Tragelaphus spekii*), have feet adapted to help them stay upright without sinking; their feet splay out to spread the weight of their body when their feet are in contact with the marshy areas in which they live.

 Talk science: balance

Have you ever lost your balance? When? Why? Have you ever walked along a thin ridge like the edge of a kerb?

 Activity: balance

Lay a tape measure or a piece of string along the floor. Ask the children if they can walk along it. Ask them: what do you do to fit your feet on the line? What do you feel like? What do you do with your arms?

Physical science and living things   141

 Talk science: tiptoes

Do you ever walk on your tiptoes? When? Why? How? Do animals walk on tiptoe?

 Activity: finding tiptoed animals

Find some still pictures and videos of four-legged animals, such as a dog, cat or horse. Better still, if you can see live animals moving, watch them. Can you see what part of their body they put on the floor? What part of this is equivalent to the part of your foot you put on the ground when walking with your whole foot? Many animals on four legs walk on tiptoes.

Balancing

The point of an object when it balances on an even surface is the centre of mass. It moves as we move so that the line of our centre of gravity is through the middle of the mass, our torso. When we stand on one leg we adjust the position of our body instinctively to do this, and this helps us to keep our balance. Other animals instinctively do the same.

Legs, which are attached to the torso, are positioned in the best place to support the weight of the body and keep it in balance. Work has been done with upper primary children about balance in a natural history museum before they were engaged in activities, they did not notice any science in action in the dioramas of animals in their respective habitats. Following activities such as those described here they could, when asked to look again, observe the science in action shown in the position of the animals. A giraffe is in this diorama but the front legs are splayed so it can bend its neck down to reach the water hole and drink (Tunnicliffe, Gazey and Gkouskou, 2015). Younger children walked on a straight line laid on the floor and were asked not to come off it. They found that they had to place their feet, one in front of the other, so as not to come off the line. They all decided to walk on tip toe and held their arms out at right angles to their sides to move and not come off the line, this way they needed to adjust their balance (Tunnicliffe and Gkouskou, 2016).

 Talk science: legs

Where are your legs? Where are the legs of a cat or dog attached to the body? Where are birds' legs attached?

Activity: how many legs

Use playdough and sticks of equal lengths to make models of four-legged and two-legged animals. How do you make the animals balance? What happens if you place the animal models on a slope? How would the animals bend to drink or sleep?

 Talk science: sinking

What happens when you walk on thick sand or snow? What happens when you walk on boggy ground? What part of an animal's body touches the sand or snow or boggy ground? Are their feet like ours or are they different? Have you ever walked on sand or snow? What was it like when you did? What did you think would happen? Why?

 Activity: making feet

You will need thick cardboard, or two layers of a thin card, scissors and glue, small tins of baked beans (to represent mass) and a sand tray or sheet of foam rubber to represent the surface of the Earth. Decide what shape of foot you are going to make, perhaps a paw like that belonging to a cat or dog, or a camel's foot. Draw a small foot of your chosen shape then make the same shape twice as big and then make another twice as big as that. Try each foot on the sand. What happens? Now add the weight of the animal. Try each foot in turn with the baked bean tin on it. What happens? What does this tell you about animals that live and move on soft surfaces? Can you make 'feet' and see how and why the camel does not sink?

Sound and light

The larger the earflap of the animal, the more sound it will collect. Nearly all mammals have ear flaps and most can move them. Have you seen one doing so? Elephants, for example, move their ears so they act as fans and allow them to lose some body heat. A bigger surface or a tube collects more sound than just a hole. The central hearing part of the ear is inside the skull. The external ear collects the sound, which makes the eardrum vibrate. So the ear flap concentrates the sound.

Physical science and living things   143

 Talk science: sound

Do all animals have ears or earflaps which you can see on the outside of their head? Some animals have large ears and some have small. Which animals do you know that have big ears compared to the size of their body? Can you hear noise easily? For some animals, being able to hear is very important to them. Why is this? Can you waggle your ears? Watch animals with earflaps move their ears. When do they move them?

 Activity: ear trumpets

Collect several plastic or paper cups and a pair of scissors. Cut a hole in the base at least 1 cm in diameter. Put your hand over one ear and put the cup base to your other ear and listen. Take the cup away. Was there a difference in the level of the sound you heard? Sometimes people prefer to have a bell rung each time to make the same level of sound to hear, so it is a fair test.

 Activity: big ears

You need: thin card, scissors, pencil and ruler, tape and string, and a sound source such as a bell or a whistle. Make a pair of big ear trumpets and make a pair of small ear trumpets. Connect each pair of ear trumpets together with the string so they can be placed on the child's head and will remain in place.

One person put on either the big ear trumpets or the small ear trumpets while another person stands in front of them (at least two metres away) and makes a sound. The person making the sound should then also stand and make noises behind and to the side of the person wearing the ear trumpets. A third person should record what the listener says about each of the sounds they can hear. Let each person have a turn and repeat the listening exercise with both sizes of ear trumpet. Can the listener always hear the sound as well when it comes from the same position whichever ears s/he is wearing? A big ear trumpet usually makes it easier to hear the sound, which appears to be louder.

Science is holistic

Living things rely on the phenomena of physics. We cannot really learn about and appreciate the living world without understanding simple ideas of physical science, only a few of which are mentioned here. Science identifies how we humans interact with one another, as that is the way the world works. It is important that young children observe these interactions and develop a holistic approach to scientific phenomena.

There are some books, such as the classic by David Attenborough (1995), which accompanied a BBC television series, *The Secret Life of Plants*, which provided further information about aspects of plants. Vogel (2009) wrote more academically about the physical world of both plants and animals; Ackerman (2016) gives a readable account of bird behaviours.

Conclusion

In many countries, physical science and biology are not effectively integrated with the child's formal learning, but the working systems of all species are governed by principles of physical science. Hearts contract producing a force which pushes fluids around the bodies of higher animals, which in turn delivers, through a physical process, oxygen to the cells, as required for the energy that keeps systems going. The shape of cells in organs are in an orpiment shape, like fitting together for the processes in which they are evolved. The movement and stability of animals on land is possible because they obey the rules of physics, such as force for locomotion and balancing on legs over their centre of mass. The physics of light affects the colours of organisms, sound is another phenomenon: the position of external ears for optimum sound wave collection reflect this aspect of physics (Tunnicliffe, Gazey and Gkouskou, 2015, Chapter 11; Tunnicliffe and Gkouskou, 2016).

This book introduces some very simple applications of physical science; it is crucial that emergent biologists are aware of physics in action in themselves and other organisms. Living things rely on the physics phenomena. We cannot really learn about and appreciate the living world without understanding these simple ideas of physical science, only a few of which are mentioned here. Science identifies the way we humans work, which is through interactions between one science area, or domain (such as physics) with another – that of biology. It is important that young children realise such interactions and hopefully develop a holistic approach to scientific phenomena. Such links are seldom made in my experience in formal teaching.

References

Ackerman, J. (2016) *The Genius of Birds*. London: Corsair.

Attenborough, D. (1995) *The Secret Life of Plants*. London: BBC Books.

Reiss, M.J. and Tunnicliffe, S.D. (2001) Students' understandings of human organs and organ systems. *Research in Science Education*, 31: 383–389.

Tunnicliffe, S.D., Gazey, R. and Gkouskou, E. (2015) Learning in physical science opportunities at natural history dioramas. In Scheersoi, A. and Tunnicliffe, S.D. (eds), *Natural History Dioramas – Traditional Exhibits for Current Educational Themes, Science Educational Aspects*. Dordrecht: Springer, pp. 171–184.

Tunnicliffe, S.D. and Gkouskou, E. (2016) HSCi physical science learning opportunities at natural history dioramas. In Costa, M.F.P.C.M., Dorrío, J.B.V., Trna, J. and Trnova, E. (eds), *Hands-on: The Heart of Science Education*. Braga: The Hands-on Science Network, pp. 1–9.

Vogel, S. (2009) *Glimpses of Creatures in Their Physical Worlds*. Princeton, NJ: Princeton University Press, p. vi.

Index

Ackerman, J. 144
action plans 6
active learning 3
adaptations 2
Agar, J. 7
age 60
Ainsworth, S. 28
'aliveness' 99–101
Allen, M. 25
amniotic fluid 82
amphibians 30, 63, 89
anatomy 2, 14–23, 32, 35
Anders, Y. 109
Anderson, S. 107
animals 25–41; big ideas 11; change and development 77–85; ears 142–143; ecological understanding 2, 104; habitats 98, 105, 106, 125; hiding 122; limbs 17; movement 25–26, 131–142, 144; naming 7, 87–89, 91–96, 99–102, 124; parasites 123–124; physical science 129, 144; seed dispersal 66; snap game 126; sun 120; taxonomic knowledge 86; *see also* birds; fish; mammals
argumentation 7, 8
Arthropods 30–31
Arthus-Bertrand, Y. 104
ash keys 74–75
assessment 90–91
Attenborough, David 144
attitudinal knowledge 4
Austin, G.A. 63, 88

babies 60–61, 62, 63, 69, 79–83
balance 140–141, 144
Bartoszeck, A.B. 55, 56
bats 29
beans 68, 72–73, 74, 75–76
bees 33, 125
beetles 30, 33–34, 77, 93
behaviours 2, 94–95
Bell, B. 101, 124

bending 136, 137
biennials 62
biodiversity 2
biological knowledge 2, 6, 27
birds: bird watch activity 108; categorisation of 89, 91, 94, 96, 102; courtship behaviour 84; drawings of 37, 38; eggs 81–82; flight 134–135; naming 7; recognition of 26
birth 60, 79, 82
bodies 14–23, 35, 81, 89, 144
bones 23, 136, 137–139; *see also* skeletons
'botaniphobia' 46
botany 44
Bradford, H. 106
Braund, M. 52
Bruner, J.S. 8, 63, 88
Brunner, M. 109
bugs 33
butterflies 30, 32, 78, 81

cacti 87, 110, 119
categorisation 50, 89–90, 91–92, 94–95, 96, 102; *see also* grouping
cells 57, 61, 81, 144
centipedes 29, 31, 78
change 45, 60–85
chordates 86, 94
chromosomes 81, 84
climate 107, 124, 126
collaboration 6, 77
colour 48, 51
communication 6, 10, 105
concepts 87, 88, 92
conkers 62
conservation 126
constructivism 5
crawling 139–140
critical thinking 77
cross-cultural perspective 27
cross-subject skills 9
crustaceans 28, 31, 36

cultural factors 29, 104
curiosity 6–7, 29

data collection 6, 10
death 100
dialogue: assessment 90–91; dialogic
    talk 5; triadic 11, 90
distaste 28, 29
dolphins 87, 132
Donaldson, M. 91, 96
drawings 9; animals 28, 30, 36, 37–39; human
    body 14–16, 17–22, 35; insects 32; plants 43,
    44, 52, 54, 55–56

ears 30, 142–143, 144
earth science 104–128
Eccles, J. 109
ecological understanding 2, 104–105
eggs 81–82, 84
embryos 82
energy 46, 135, 144
environment 47, 106–108, 124
Ergazaki, M. 6
erosion 111, 112–113
everyday activities 1–2
evolution 81

Fančovičová, J. 16, 17
feet 140, 142
ferns 84
fish 28–29, 32; bones 137; categorisation
    of 89, 92, 96; drawings of 37, 38
Fleer, M. 5
flight 134–135
flowers 48, 51–52, 53, 124; big ideas 11;
    categorisation of 96; movement 131;
    shapes 47, 49–50
foetuses 82, 83
food 46–47, 50, 53, 57, 58
friction 133
fungi 48, 57–58, 124

gardening 44, 52
gardens 51–52
Gastropods 31
gender differences 79
giant redwood 67
Goodnow, J.J. 63, 88
Gopnik, A. 7
Goulart, M.I.M. 6
grouping 88–89, 91–92, 94, 96, 102; see also
    categorisation
growth: humans 82; plants
    63–65, 67, 68–69, 73–74,
    76–77, 129–131
gut 34, 37

habitats 27, 98, 105, 108, 123–125; activities 106;
    conservation 126; ecological understanding 2,
    104; plants 54; soil 110, 113; wetlands 107
Henriques, L. 108, 117
hiding 122
Hilson, C. 107–108
'hole through the middle' 34–35
holistic approach 143–144
home, learning at 22, 23
house plants 44, 52
Hughes, M. 7
human body see bodies

i-spy 97
ice 111–112
imagination 8, 95
imitation 5
Inagaki, K. 32
inferential knowledge 4
informal learning 1
Inhelder, B. 89
inquiry 44
insects 29, 30, 32, 33–34, 47, 84
interpretation 42, 86, 108
invertebrates 29, 32, 36–37; movement 78;
    observation of 27–28; outside body pattern
    30–31; recognition of 33–34; use of the
    word 86
investigation 6, 7, 10

jellyfish 34, 135, 136
Jenkins, D. 42, 44
Jewell, N.M. 101

Keil, F. 92, 95
Kellert, S.R. 29
knowledge: anatomy 22–23, 35; animals 77;
    biological 2, 6, 27; embedded 93; plants 44;
    taxonomic 86; trees 56; types of 4
Korfiatis, K. 25

labelling 2, 89–90; see also naming
ladybirds 33–34, 48
Lakoff, G. 95
Langer, S.K. 8
language 2, 6, 86, 96, 105; see also naming;
    vocabulary
larvae 77, 78, 93
learning: active 3; animals 25–26, 27–28; learning
    environment 9; naming 91–92; out of school
    22, 23; play 4–5
leaves 48, 65–67, 95
legs 141–142
life and death 100–101
life circles 63, 78, 80
life cycle 61–62

light 76–77, 120–121, 129, 144
limbs 17, 23, 137
Linn, M.N. 5
lions 89
listening 25, 143
literacy 6, 25
Louv, R. 46, 106
Lucas, A.M. 96

malaria 123
mammals 27, 30; categorisation of 89, 96; developing babies 81, 82; drawings of 37–39; language use 96; naming 87; parental care 68
maps 27
Markman, E. 87
mass 140, 141
maths 11–12
mating 81, 83–84
mealworms 27–28, 77, 78, 93, 139
media 44
mental models 17
metamorphosis 63, 77
minibeasts 33, 86
Mintzes, J.J. 87
misconceptions 2, 8
molluscs 31, 139–140
moon 123
Moss, B. 107
mould 57
movement 46, 78, 100; animals 25–26, 131–142, 144; plants 129–130
Mung beans 72–73, 74, 75–76
muscles 23, 135, 136
mushrooms 57–58

naming 7, 11, 12, 16, 50, 86–103, 115, 124; see also vocabulary
narratives 7, 8
National Curriculum 19
Native Americans 104
nature 46, 104, 106
'new life' 78–81
night 123
numeracy 5, 6, 11–12, 17, 25, 48–49

observation 9, 86; of animals 28–29, 30; earth science 108; plants 45
Opperman, E. 109
organs/organ systems 18–23, 31–32, 35, 144
out of school learning 22
owls 30

parasites 123–124
parents 23, 68, 84, 108
Partain, V. 28

Patrick, P. 27, 46
pebbles 114
pendulum movement 132–133
penguins 132
perennials 62
personal biological knowledge 6
personalisation 42
pets 31–32, 39
Philips, W.C. 106, 117
photo journals 10–11
photographs 26, 45, 102
photosynthesis 66, 67
physical science 129–144
physics 4, 129, 143, 144
physiology 2
Piaget, J. 89, 117
pine cones 48, 84
place 106, 108
Plakitsi, K. 6
'plant blindness' 46, 52, 96, 124
plant walk journals 45
plants 39, 42–59, 124; big ideas 11; germination 66–67; growth 63–65, 67, 68–69, 73–74, 76–77, 129–131; life circles 63; movement 129–130; naming 50, 87–89, 91–102; parasites 124; parental care 68; physical science 129, 144; reproduction and development 61–62, 65, 81, 83–84; seed dispersal 66, 119, 129–130; soil 110; sun 119, 125; taxonomic knowledge 86; see also seeds
play 2, 4–6
pollination 81, 84, 119, 125
pollution 125–126
predators 29
pregnancy 79
problem solving 4, 5, 77
procedural knowledge 4
Prokop, M. 29, 31
Prokop, P. 16, 17, 29, 31
puberty 79

questioning 7–8, 11

rain 117
reading 6, 25
record keeping 9–10
Rega-Brodsky, C. 107–108
Reiss, M.J.: children's understanding of the body 16, 19; children's views of living organisms 25; drawings of animals 55; ecological understanding 104–105; human organs 35; invertebrates 36; 'plant blindness' 52; skeletons 138; vertebrates 29, 37
reproduction 53, 62, 65, 78–80, 81, 83–84
reptiles 89, 90–91
rewilding 125

rhymes 14, 98
rocks 109, 110, 111–112, 115
roots 47, 51, 53, 74, 129
Rosenfeld, S. 96
Roth, W.-M. 6
Rybska, E. 29, 55, 56

Sajkowska, Z.A. 55, 56
sand dunes 110
Sanders, D. 42, 44, 52
Schneekloth, L.H. 46
Schussler, E. 109
science 4; earth 104–128; narratives 8; physical
    129–144; talking 8–9
scientific literacy 25
seedlings 53, 64, 76–77
seeds 53, 58, 65–67; activities 62, 64, 68, 69–77,
    101–102; 'aliveness' 101; life cycle 61–62;
    pollination 84; wind dispersal 119, 129–130
self-regulation 4
sense of place 106
sequoia 67
sex cells 61, 81
sex education 78, 79–80
shadows 120–121
shapes 5, 11–12, 47, 48–50, 51, 52
shrimps 27–28, 84
Simmons, D.A. 124
size 12; babies 83; classification of objects 89;
    particles 113; plants 42–43
skeletons 16, 18, 19, 23, 100, 135–136, 138–139
skills 7, 9
slugs 29, 31, 78, 139
smells 48, 51, 95
snails 31, 37, 78, 139–140
snakes 29, 91, 122, 132, 136
snap 126
soil 109–111, 112–114, 124, 126, 129
sound 142–143, 144
SPACE (Science Processes and Concept
    Exploration) project 109
sperm 81, 84
spiders 29, 30–31
stars 123
stopping 134
storytelling 7
Sumida, M. 107
sun 52, 119–120, 121, 125, 131
sweetcorn 67
swimming 132
sycamore keys 74–75
symbols 26, 43, 117–118
Symington, D. 9, 15

tadpoles 77, 78
talking 6, 8–9, 25

tapeworms 123
taxonomy 2, 50, 86, 87, 89, 91–93, 96; *see also*
    categorisation; grouping
team work 77
temperature 76
testimonial knowledge 4
Their, H. 5
time 60
time-telling 121
tiptoes 141
Tizard, B. 7
Torkar, G. 30
Tough, J. 7, 86
training 23
trees 42, 43, 46, 53, 55–57; age of 64;
    categorisation of 48, 89, 96–97
triadic dialogue 11, 90
Trowbridge, J.E. 87
Tunnicliffe, S.D.: 'botaniphobia' 46; children's
    understanding of the body 16, 17, 19;
    children's views of living organisms 25;
    ecological understanding 104–105; human
    organs 35; invertebrates 29, 36; pets 31; plants
    51, 55, 56; skeletons 138; vertebrates 37
Tversky, B. 91
Tytler, R. 28

Unsworth, S.J. 104

vegetables 50, 51, 58, 68, 96
vegetation 46, 47, 52, 107, 110, 124
vertebrates 18, 29–30, 31–32, 37–38, 86, 94, 137
Villabi, R.M. 96
Villaroel, J.D. 52
vocabulary 12, 44, 47, 107, 109; *see also* naming
Vogel, S. 129, 144

walking 131–132, 133, 141
Wandersee, J. 109
Warren, P.S. 107–108
waste 34
water 121–122; erosion 112–113; ice 111–112;
    plants 53, 55, 56–57, 119; seeds 66, 68, 72–73,
    75–76; swimming animals 132; water birds 135
water snails 139–140
weather 107, 116–118, 126
welfare 2
Westervelt, M.O. 29
wetlands 107
whales 87, 132
Whitebread, D. 4
wind 66, 117, 118–119, 121–122, 129
woodlice 29, 78
word searches 98
worms 29, 30, 31, 33, 36–37, 135, 136, 139
writing 25